The Edge of the City

The Edge of the City

A SCRAPBOOK
1976–91

DESMOND HOGAN

The Lilliput Press
DUBLIN

First published in Ireland
by The Lilliput Press Limited
4 Rosemount Terrace, Arbour Hill, Dublin 7

A CIP record for this book is
available from the British Library

ISBN 1 874675 03 1

The Lilliput Press receives financial assistance from
The Arts Council/An Chomhairle Ealaíon, Ireland

Photoset by Wilmaset Ltd, Wirral
Printed in Great Britain by
Clays Ltd, St Ives plc

For Joachim Sartorius and Karin Kiwus
from the bits and pieces of Kreuzberg I try to build again

Auch in abnehmender Frist, auch in den Wochen der Wendung.
Niemand verhulfe uns jewieder zum Vollsein,
Als der einsame wigene Gang uber der schlaflosen Landschaft.

Not in a waning phase, nor yet in the weeks of versation
Would there be ever one to help us to fullness again,
Save for our own lone walk over the sleepless land.

Rainer Maria Rilke

CONTENTS

AUTHOR'S NOTE

These bits and pieces I've written for music papers, women's magazines, national newspapers, English and Irish, over the years. Many had to fit into journalistic expectations. Some didn't. They are mostly records of places, some are reactions to writers, some encounters with people. Years when I was writing fiction there is little or nothing. Other years there is much. Taken collectively they create a scrapbook, a diary, a journey. The scrapbook begins in autumn 1976 when I went to San Francisco from Dublin. There were roses of Sharon by tramlines that autumn and Hare Krishna monks all over the city with orange balloons. By a Victorian house with an owlish face I found a diagram illustrating the horrors of Hell. I never really returned to Dublin after San Francisco. In a sense I wandered. From address to address in London. London is a city of cheap flights and when I had money I used it for that. The bits and pieces begin to cohere and they become a solid diary, a place to speak to, to call back people encountered in foreign cities I may never meet again, with whom there was a conversation in which neither of us could fathom what the other was saying but its import, at least for me, always there, a companion who gives me courage when my own courage fails.

Soho Square Gardens
30 March 1991

ACKNOWLEDGEMENTS

These pieces have appeared in the following magazines and newspapers and have been published in the books and by the publishers I acknowledge:

In Dublin, *Hot Press*, *New Statesman*, *Books and Bookmen*, *That Lady* (Virago; Viking Penguin, New York), *Image*, *The Independent*, *Sunday Times*, *Thirty-Two Counties* (Secker & Warburg), *Sunday Tribune*, *Irish Press*, *European Gay Review*, *Evening Standard*, *The Times*, *Mirabella*, *Krino*, *Storm*, *Cork Review*, *Irish Ways*, *Graph*.

Dates refer to the time that the pieces were written.

1976

Santa Cruz

It was a big jamboree – it reminded me of English circuses which
visited Ireland when I was a child. They sold ice cream, they sold
Dr Peppers, they sold sheets of poetry written by young women
who alleged they rose at six to perform motherhood rites. This
was Santa Cruz's fourth annual poetry festival.

The festival was the high point of an Indian summer which
glorified the white Italianate villas of this town with their louvred
shutters, which turned side streets to gold, side streets which
very often ended at clusters of copper-leaf bushes.

Occasionally languid-limbed young men and young women
wandered on the beach. The waters were warmer than Salthill in
July but no one seemed to venture in except me. There were
always the surfers though, a monotony on the Californian scene
by now. In San Francisco I'd met many young people who'd
come from the dark city of Dublin a few years before. They'd
stayed on, 'attracted by the call of Atlantis' one of them told me.

California was a trail of seaside towns for me. Westport in
northern California where all the activity seemed to be at the
filling station and where a lackadaisical dog kept an eye on the
sea. Mendocino from where you can see the grey whales go
south, where white clapboard houses look to the surf dynamit-
ing against rocks, where young people convene around the *I
Ching* in a logwood health-food café.

But in Santa Cruz the sun catches the chords of guitars at
evening.

Optimism has its victims. About ten people each summer are
murdered. There's a nearby valley where the Indians would

3

never go, they'd just spy on it from the hills. It was a favourite of Charles Manson and his disciples.

These nights, nights of November, a fog hangs over Santa Cruz, a serene, disciplined wraith. Elsewhere the night is clear, with sidereal bulwarks over the Pacific.

'He that increaseth knowledge increaseth sorrow,' a sign had said in the window of a caravan north of Westport.

A middle-aged woman with Indian braids, in an orange dress with gold slabs on it, walked through the fog to the festival.

A young lady appeared on stage. It was her first public appearance. We were told she was shy. She looked at us directly. Her face was a clear, tremulous face.

> recalling the times
> when love leaps
> in my chest
> like a fish.

Her voice has a lilt one hears all the time in California, the lilt of poesy, the excess of anguish. The MC has it. She announces the poets as if they're the subjects of therapy. Jimmy Lyons from Greenwich Village takes giant prowling steps on.

> Sweet
> Street
> Poet
> Greenwich
> Village.

William Everson wears a cowboy hat. His white hair is long. His shoulders are penitent. He became a Catholic, then a monk, wrote under the name Brother Antoninus, fell in love with a nun. They applied to the Pope to live in celibate circumstances together. Permission refused. He moved in with her anyway. He speaks of the weather at Big Sur, the sudden calamitous storm.

William Burroughs is led on. He gives us a dark look. His voice is a monotonous drawl. Young people cheer when he finishes. He looks at them sadly. This generation took his son.

He loves Santa Cruz he says. Narrow streets, Spanish architecture, a quietude in the streets at night. A poster of Walt Whitman, in a slouch hat, in bravado pose, over a sofa in a bookstore which is still open. Outside red roses for sale.

After William Burroughs two Indian dancers come on and perform like flamingos until something goes amiss with the Indian music and then, hands on their hips, they start a slagging match with the music co-ordinator.

It is John Klemmer I will remember. We are all swept into the baroque, talkative tones of his saxophone.

A few days later outside a café, within a white pen, a jazz band plays. The sun is going down. People come from nowhere with balloons. They bounce the balloons in the air. The movements of their arms are slow, balletic. The balloons seem to multiply. The sun is red. A few teenagers on skateboards sail in among the balloon bouncers. The sun is getting redder and the balloons bouncier. An old lady, hair in a grey and white bun, curled up in a pale blue dress, stares.

The balloons and the young people disappear. The salt air is bitter and laden. Tomorrow it will be another place, more translucent waves.

On arriving in San Francisco I met a young man from New York in Gino and Carlo's pub who'd read an old *Life* magazine article on the Beat poets and had hitched all the way to San Francisco, hoping to spot some. He had blond hair and wore a pea-green jacket. He was staying in a tiny, roach-ridden room.

And I think in Santa Cruz: the survival of idealism is always possible if you dip deep enough and are rewarded with the right words, the right gestures, words and gestures born of personal discovery.

1977

Cairo

The sun is Hell. It is July, the hottest month. Even the Egyptians sweat. Europeans look helpless. The nights throb with the beat of drums or bleat with sagpipes. Late into the night there are wedding parties consulting along the banks of the Nile.

During the day couples take off in lateens. Cars tear across bridges, horns savagely beeping. Gurkies, white towel-like robes thrown around them, run among the cars and sometimes the stealthier ones run in front of cars. One-legged men lie against the walls of houses. A bedlam of people bow to the sun. A goat comes to a parapet above a bank to have a look. Women, behind yashmaks, sell Pepsi Cola every few yards along the Nile while hens strut beside them and enthralling children wander. Every morning you wake to the muezzin's cry of 'Allah'.

Yesterday I went to the desert, climbed the biggest pyramid, drank sugar-cane juice when I came back down, hallucinated. Horsemen rode by in the desert in front of me.

Cairo is the ancient city of Babylon. Jews still have an enclave to which Joseph fled and where Moses was found. They live there among flocks of goats. The streets are dizzying, sometimes maiming with goats, hens, fruit, the destitute, children, Pepsi Cola dealers. Then, on the Nile, a peach sail evokes the Bible.

In the old part of Cairo a limousine draws up and a man with an old public-schoolboy's accent, his pate a raging red, asks me the way to the British war cemetery. By the Nile a fat man from Alexandria asks me for a photograph and I give him a youth hostel one.

This indeed is the land of Isis, Mother Goddess. As I write, already night, cars scream and jangle past, part of a wedding.

Cameras flash by the waters of Babylon. The brides have phosphorescent black hair and their dresses are snowflake white and their lipstick liquid crimson.

In Dublin, just before I left it, a woman had a catatonic fit at a party, screaming at me, denouncing me with every obscenity she could think of.

Happiness comes from nowhere. Maybe it's the Goddess Isis speaking, telling me to go on.

1980

Margaretta D'Arcy and John Arden

The Non-Stop Connolly Show was first performed in Dublin on the evening of 29 March 1975, Easter Saturday. Many people attended this vigil, not just socialists and Republicans but young people who had long tired of trying to make something out of their history. Margaretta D'Arcy and John Arden had shaped a spectacle from the life and times of James Connolly, Irish socialist leader; they also helped produce it and took part in it. The show, six parts in all, was supposed to last twenty-four hours. That was legendary. It finished appropriately about seven in the morning on the stage of Liberty Hall, Dublin, amid a swish of flags, orange and green. The irony was unmistakable. It was at Easter week-end 1916 that men marched from Liberty Hall, Dublin, Connolly among others, to occupy the GPO among other places, to add to the perennial catalogue of rebellions in Irish history.

For those of us who took part in the show it was a night we'd been working towards for virtually three months. Actors, young and old, playwrights, socialists, musicians. Arden and D'Arcy had picked at random from around Dublin and like Pied Pipers had collected people who couldn't have been more different in background, politics or commitment. There were film shows between acts, songs. One heard a girl's lament in Gaelic between episodes which debated Ireland's right to independence from England or showed supporters of Eugene Debs's presidential campaign running around the hall, imitating a train.

I played most notably Matt Talbot, Dublin proletarian mystic who tied himself in chains and lacerated himself with whips to redeem Dublin of its sins; Sean O'Casey, Dublin's poetic drama-tist; Francis Sheehy Skeffington, an elegant pacifist and feminist.

I remember the cold of the hall, the determination of the actors, the dynamic climax of the play: the dramatic dilemma of Connolly, would he or would he not join the nationalist revolution?

There was an uncanny tension which locked these scenes together, a poignancy for those of us who were educated on the sanctity of 1916. D'Arcy and Arden are the only dramatists I know of to focus on this central crux of Irish history through historical characters; what is the position of a socialist in the face of an overwhelmingly nationalistic sense of history?

There were many uprisings in Irish history, all sung about or celebrated in doggerel verse. Ireland has two traditions: one not so much of the gun but of vicious, merciless violence, the scythe, the sword, the bomb; the other the pacifist tones of someone like Daniel O'Connell, the like of whom strikes a deeper chord in the Irish psyche.

Connolly came from neither tradition. He was a Republican and a socialist who loathed Pearse's blood-lust – 'The old heart of the earth needed to be warmed with the red wine of the battlefield' – but who ultimately opted for a bloody revolution on a minor scale not so much to break from Britain but to let out his own protest against Britain's centuries of manhandling Ireland.

The end of *The Non-Stop Connolly Show* has a verve, an alacrity, a triumphant tenacity with words that is elsewhere missing in the play. One feels one is in the presence of great drama and that the drama was made from a cold eye, an eye which like Yeats's, penetrated lies, phobias, images which dressed other images, and came up with – even if only for moments at a stretch – a mind-boggling authenticity.

The first production of the play was lit with colour, masks, flashes of crazy cartoon wit; would one forget Queen Victoria's Jubilee procession, for instance? Or a very arch-looking doll who resembled Pope Pius XII being carried across the stage earnestly pursued by a goonish W. B. Yeats and a Maud Gonne who was much his senior?

Staring at a bald script, though from a vantage of five years later, I confess boredom, frustration with much of the material.

The efforts to make Connolly and his relatives illustrious fall flat a lot of the time; there is a niggling veniality, a lack of drive, a supposition of audience awareness of contemporary political arguments.

However that point is far transcended by the dynamics of the play as it reaches its crucial stages. Parts 1,2,3,4 cover the biographical necessities of Connolly's career. Parts 5 and 6 show Connolly in conflict with two of the major Irish political figures of the time, Jim Larkin, the trade union leader and self-made messiah, and Patrick Pearse, the principled, eclectic Irish nationalist. And wedded to these confrontations are the background issues of the time – war, hunger, strikes, more than anything the lockout of 1913 and the Great War. At these points, points that assail the dignity of the human being in immediate terms, the dramatists excel themselves. There is a wonderful grasp of dialect, of historical incident, of the odd revealing piece of poetry. The use of English is resonant, always clear, and flowing. A few lines sum up a battle. A phrase evokes an era.

A mystic emerges in the middle of a storm of aggression, an English suffragette wonders at the intransigence of Ireland, Larkin summons the Dublin proletariat to a side street, the shoulders of a God on him, the arm of a soldier, a war demon does a pirouette and renders an account of the horrors of the First World War, Connolly in his execution chair looks back on his life and refuses to apologize, not even to his own fragmented conscience.

One is reminded of the early Arden, of *Sergeant Musgrave's Dance* and *Armstrong's Last Goodnight*, a firm purpose, a refusal to stand on soggy ground. The landscapes of the play are more D'Arcy's I suspect, the gnomish politicians, the tirelessly ugly capitalists, the proletariat rallying, asking for manna. John Arden is an English writer who came to live in Ireland. Margaretta D'Arcy is of Irish and Russian Jewish origins. Together they moulded the finest interpretation of Irish history ever achieved dramatically.

That the Irish nation seemed to reject their gift is not surprising. Ireland is as it was in Yeats's time:

The beating down of the wise
And great Art beaten down.

The National Theatre of Ireland and the National Theatre of Britain made no overtures to the Ardens.

After the production in Dublin some five years ago we toured Ireland. Firstly we went North. Numbers quickly dwindled and we were left with a few who ended up reading the plays to small but fascinated audiences. We stayed with Billy MacMillen, the Offical Sinn Fein leader, four days before he was shot dead. We journeyed to Galway, perhaps seven of us left then, including two of the Arden children. That was the most successful part of the production, those readings; there was an immediacy, a lack of pomp that lent itself to the Arden proselytism.

Margaretta D'Arcy and John Arden were organizers of the recent tribunal on the British presence in the north of Ireland. In that capacity they invited me as an Irish writer also living outside Ireland to read some of my work at an entertainment to finance this tribunal. I accepted their invitation because, although I am an enemy of the vicious violence that passes in Northern Ireland as tactics of liberation, I believe with one of the patrons of the tribunal, Noel Browne, for instance, that the British army are exacerbating violence in areas where there wouldn't otherwise be any. However, some days before the entertainment I was told I couldn't go because certain people had objected to remarks I'd made about violence at a seminar in the ICA. After some wrangling I went anyway, read to red-hot Republicans and interested English people passages from my novel about an Irish woman looking for a wayward son in England.

But it is Connolly who must have the last word. As James Stephens said, 'If Larkin was the magnetic centre of the Irish labour movement, Connolly was its brains.' It was those brains which were addled when confronted with Pearse's fanaticism and violent wishes. Yet it was Connolly who founded the Irish Labour party which has included such diverse members as Noel Browne and Conor Cruise O'Brien, one who forever reminds us of the conflict in Irish minds between the two manifest Irish traditions, that of violence and that of constitutional agitation. Connolly mutters towards the end of the play:

> Out in the street the people throng and rush
> And cry aloud 'Bread, bread, where is our food –
> This child destroys our life,' they cry.
> It would not have been done had there been another way.

Was there another way? Sean O'Casey would have said yes. Francis Sheehy Skeffington would have said yes. But for Margaretta D'Arcy and John Arden it's an emphatic no, and we are reminded at the end of the play of their present concerns with the island to which they have given so much dedication. As Connolly is strapped into his seat of execution, a wounded man, his thoughts veer on Ireland:

> They always claimed that they were here to stay.
> They did not ask us if they may.
> And altogether they asked so very few
> That when the fire and sword and fury flew
> At them in Russia, China, Cuba, Africa, Vietnam
> And indeed once more in Ireland, my own home,
> They could not credit what it was they'd done.

I have no doubt that Margaretta D'Arcy and John Arden will continue illuminating areas that most of us don't want to think about, let alone talk about; it is our privilege to contradict them but theirs to write about H-blocks, Armagh gaol, the cancerous conditions of Irish political prisoners in English gaols, to go on saying over and over again that people have a right to stand up to the system and that those fighting oppression with their nerves are considerably aided by those who fight with the pen.

1983

Sources of happiness in the work of Mary Lavin

A fitting introduction to the work of Mary Lavin might be an emblem from a mesmeric and lonely short story by one of her contemporaries, Eudora Welty, 'The Bride of the Innisfallen', a story of journeying and estrangement and newness, the newness of place, and the newness of self away from familiar surroundings and ingrained relationships. 'You must never betray pure joy – the kind you were born and began with – either by hiding it or by parading it in front of people's eyes; they didn't want to be shown it. And still you must tell it.' With the republication by Virago in April of Mary Lavin's second and last novel, *Mary O'Grady*, and the recent publication by Constable of the third volume of Mary Lavin's stories, it would seem an appropriate moment to take a bold look at the work of Mary Lavin and its unifying obsession with happiness and inner life; the fierce admonition her work seems to give that inner life should be protected at all costs. One of her most complete later stories, contained in Volume Three of her collected stories, is in fact called 'Happiness', and in this the heroine who has forged a path through all of her volumes of stories is prostrate and dying, seeing psychic daffodils on the bedroom floor. 'Her theme was happiness: what it was, what it was not; where we might find it, where not; and how, if found, it must be guarded.' The opening of 'Happiness' could be an appraisal of Mary Lavin's lifetime struggle. Frank O'Connor's description of Mary Lavin is not altogether different. 'Like Whitman's wild oak in Louisiana, she has stood a little apart from the rest of us "uttering joyous leaves of dark green"'. *Mary O'Grady*, first published in 1950 when Mary Lavin had already published three volumes of stories and one novel, written in a month while her father was dying, is unusually frenetic among her work, a series of mosaics, a description of family, an attempted analysis of family relationships, and particularly a portrait of an Irish mother who consumes joys and tragedies, rewards and afflictions into the treadmill of Irish motherhood which eventually entitles her to a beatific vision of an Elysium, not unlike the fields of Tullamore which she exiled herself from to be an Irish mother and widow in Dublin. 'There are only two valid relationships, blood and passion,' one of Mary Lavin's stories insists and *Mary O'Grady* makes short shrift of anything that does not come into the realm of blood and passion. It seems in this novel that anyone, like the son Patrick, who does not bow to these twin authorities is destroyed by their profligacy. The biographical fact that *Mary O'Grady* was written while Mary Lavin's father was dying is more than interesting for it is a father character, in various shades, who provides most surprises in her work. In *The Shrine*, 1977, there is a story called 'Tom' in which a father writes a letter in aberrant English to his daughter, on pink paper, on the eve of the Grand National.

> You Seem to wait till the Ball Came to you that is Rong you should Keep Moving and and Not to Stay in the One Place. God Luck,
>
> > Dadey.

In Mary Lavin's work there are people who move and people who are still – like Mary O'Grady – people trapped by stillness and people obliterated by movement – like the son Patrick in *Mary O'Grady*. But it is not so much the darers who have Mary Lavin's admiration as those whose state of either movement or stillness comes from complex, integral decisions. Miss Lomas in 'The Mock Auction' and Vera in 'One Summer' are among those who are still and yet achieve felicity, despite the contradictions, in their stillness.

One of those who went the furthest is Lally in an early story, 'The Will'. She went from Athenry to Dublin, the 'heart of that mystery', is spurned by her mother for making a bad marriage and for sinking so low as to have lodgers, is cut out of the will. But Lally realizes that, despite the revulsion of her family towards her, 'You were you always, no matter where you went or what you did . . . you don't change', and so makes a manifesto for the Irish artist in declining a compromised family offer of money to her. She anticipates Edna O'Brien's personal and grieved manifesto in *Mother Ireland*: 'Those who feel and go along with the journey of their feelings are richer than the seducers who hit and run.' Instead of taking money she sinks her own pittances into lighting 'some holy lamps at the Convent of Perpetual Reparation', for her mother died in bitterness and non-forgiveness towards her.

Someone who is forgiven but too late is the happy-go-lucky young man in the magnificent 'The Little Prince', driven across the 'vast Atlantic' because he is a spendthrift. 'Many a young man like him went out in danger to come home a different man altogether; a man to be respected: a well-to-do man with a fur lining in his top coat, his teeth stopped with gold, and the means to hire motor cars and drive his relatives about the countryside.' Years later his sister makes the same journey to try to find him only to come up in her searchings with a corpse which might or might not be him. 'But if it was her brother something had sundered them, something had severed the bonds of blood, and she knew him not. And if it was I who was lying there, she thought, he wouldn't know me. It signified nothing that they might once have sprung from the same womb. Now they were strangers.' The myth of blood bonds is unassailably contested. A strange room is opened in Irish fiction. The rage is Faulknerian. There is no rest for the conscience in Athenry.

The middle stories are concerned with efforts to protect the self and inner life against the loneliness of the body, against incursions from strangers, against an obtusely unsympathetic society. A 'dowdy, lumpish and unromantic figure' wanders through these stories, often stumbling on unexpected moments of triumph, unexpected epiphanies composed from everyday details. The story 'Happiness' seems to obliterate this heroine, as if the struggle has gone on long enough, and acknowledgement of ultimate triumph is made with a deathbed scene in which a mother finally communicates to a hitherto uncomprehending daughter her Tolstoyan vision of happiness – 'Nor think sorrow its exact opposite' – thus preserving the continuity of things, injecting a personal vision into the family tree, sublimating the self into the general. In a very recent story, 'A Bevy of Aunts', in her most recent volume, *A Family Likeness*, two 'fragile, gilded' Italian chairs, once belonging to the narrator's aunts, are passed on to the narrator's daughters, thus acting as a metaphor for happy continuity, for, as it were, Yeats's 'spreading laurel tree'. Mary O'Grady doesn't let go of life until she knows her youngest daughter Rosie is pregnant, thus family continuity preserved. The nightmare of self is dissolved in the omnipotent family tree. But this, I would suggest, is a longing more than a reality in her work. One of Mary Lavin's saddest stories is another recent one, 'Eterna', in which a doctor befriends a nun who has become a nun because the nuns were the only people who ever took an interest in her, showing her she could paint. Years after their friendship the doctor sights a strange, wrecked creature in the National Gallery in Dublin whom he presumes to be that nun. 'People had to clip their wings if they wanted to survive in this world,' he smugly remarks, recalling the nun's one-time embarrassing idealism, thus echoing Sean O'Faolain's statement 'It's a terrible and lovely thing to look at the face of death when you are young but it unfits a man for the long humiliation of life.'

The fundamental and integral mood in Mary Lavin's work, however, is not of effulgent happiness or of spiritual contraction. For all the priests and nuns and brothers who inhabit it it is agnostic. It seems to say, at its most intense and unhindered, 'I don't know.'

To get to the heart of this fiction we visit the midlands of Ireland and one summer when a father, who may have killed his wife and who has permanently destroyed a romantic relationship of his daughter's, is dying, tended by his daughter.

'When they dig the black hole and put you down in it that's the end of you.'

'Oh no!' Vera's heart cried out against the thought of facing into that nothingness, that nowhere. 'Of course there is a hereafter,' she cried. 'Otherwise what would be the meaning of love?'

Weak tears came into his eyes. 'Do you really believe that, Vera?' he said.

Partly lying and, like himself, partly wanting to believe it, she nodded.

He closed his eyes. 'It would make up for everything,' he added, almost under his breath. Then he opened his eyes wide. 'Just to see her. Just to see her again is all I'd ask.'

Vera's own eyes widened. 'Who are you talking about?'

'Your mother,' he said, and he looked surprised. 'Who else?'

The power of 'One Summer' is overwhelming. As in many of Mary Lavin's stories the statement is by a total, pure, almost girl-like artist. You can see all the inchoate lives, the brothers, the priests, the nuns, the celibate lawyers, the state of lack of knowledge, and the woman in the café off Grafton Street whose only life statement, when it comes to the crunch, can be: 'I'm lonely. Are you?'

1984

Kate O'Brien:
her life in the writing

Why did'st thou promise such a beauteous day
And make me travel forth without my cloak?

Between her birth in Boru House, Limerick, on 3 December 1897 and her death in the Kent and Canterbury Hospital, Canterbury, in the afternoon of 13 August 1974, Kate O'Brien chose discretion and privacy as a maxim for her life. In her last book, a book of reminiscences, *Presentation Parlour* (1963), Kate O'Brien piquantly refers to an aunt, a nun, who expressed a desire to read her first novel *Without My Cloak* (1931) and was only given it with certain sections pinned by safety pins. The nun was amply satisfied with her censored read. In a way, when one comes to look at it, unlike those of many authors, certain sections of Kate O'Brien's life are closed off from us by safety pins. To know a little more one must construct from the pointers in her fiction, from her few autobiographical writings; one asks her friends, one delicately handles an heirloom of photographs.

My favourite photograph of Kate is one of her in her twenties, about the time of her short-lived marriage, in a shapeless many-coloured jersey. She has a face that resembles someone she quoted in *English Diaries and Journals* (1943), Katherine Mansfield. A face that is both serene and yet dogged by the fact of exile. It is an image that is premature in a final reckoning with Kate O'Brien because the image of her that seems to survive is that of the author of *That Lady*; her public portrait was finally completed with the success of *That Lady*, a middle-aged woman still with a 1920s-style hair cut, her impressively boned Limerick face a little solemn, her eyes aristocratic, challenging, but not arrogant.

Having spent a while looking at Kate O'Brien's work my conclusion is that she was incapable of arrogance. Her life, like her work, was a supplication to a God who was partly provincial and partly a global traveller.

In her life Kate O'Brien knew the vicissitudes of poverty and wealth; she encountered international success and in the latter part of her life on The Street, Boughton in Kent, an eclipse from the public eye. In many ways the end of *That Lady* was prophetic of the end of Kate O'Brien. As Ana de Mendoza forfeits her Mantegna, a lifetime of refinement enshrined in it, so we can presume Kate had to relinquish her own precious works of art on selling her house in Roundstone, Connemara (a house recently owned and vacated by Sting of The Police) and retiring to Kent. But prior to this fate, as for Ana de Mendoza, the mulberry trees had bloomed for Kate, the world of her time had chattered about her, as in the cases of Rose and Clare in *As Music and Splendour* she was more than familiar with the 'symbols and augurs of total success'.

Kate O'Brien's grandfather was evicted from a small farm just after the Famine; he headed towards Limerick city where by the 1860s he had established a thriving horse-breeding business. In her first novel *Without My Cloak*, a grand gesture of an Irish novel not unlike Eilís Dillon's recent *Across the Bitter Sea*, Kate chronicled the emotional lives of an Irish bourgeois family through the nineteenth century. But Irish bourgeois families, as in the case of Kate's own, very often have their roots in recent poverty and catatonic acts of transcendence. Insecurity travels like a banshee through such families. In her second novel, *The Ante-Room* (1934), a kind of *Lady Chatterley's Lover* without the release of the sexual act, Kate very brilliantly, very toughly denuded such a family of the romance and left us with images of the detritus of the Irish bourgeois family, the gardens, the garden-houses, the guns poised for suicide.

Kate's much-loved mother died when Kate was a child and she was sent to Laurel Hill Convent, run by the Faithful Companions of Jesus, which she left when she was eighteen. Kate loved the school, a school where Mother Thecla and the bishop were wont to converse in Latin in the garden, a school which bordered on the magisterial Shannon, and from it she coaxed the experience for her most perfect novel, *The Land of Spices* (1941), one of the most important smaller novels of the twentieth century. Youth is set against age. A girl on the threshold of life against a nun about to become Mother General of her order. There is love between nun and girl. But intercepting this love, in the nun's eyes, is an image of her father making love to a boy student in Brussels, a sight which initially drove her into the convent. The innocence of age and the innocence of youth is intercepted by an image of carnal love. The girl is walking into the world of such images. The nun is quietly withdrawing from the memory of the image. We can take it that Kate, on leaving Laurel Hill in June 1916, was walking into the world of these paradoxes, innocence inaugurated into experience. The nun was based on an English Reverend Mother who was at Laurel Hill in Kate's time, a woman who never smiled, so alienated was she by this grey city and this to her slovenly river, a woman of 'Yorkshire bred and Stonyhurst men'.

Already the duality of Ireland and England was established in Kate's personality. An American writers' directory of the 1940s tells us that on Kate's visit to the United States in the late 1940s she was without an Irish accent. I imagine those pinched 'Stonyhurst' eyes looking with trepidation after Kate from a convent gate in 1916. Kate's father died in 1916. His business had already been in decline. In Dublin in her mackintosh, 'half starved by the holy men and the holy women', Kate walked among the ruins of an English-built city. An uncle of hers, Uncle Hickey, had wept when Queen Victoria, 'our great little queen', had died. But Kate befriended many young and radiant revolutionaries at University College, a great number of whom, she tells us, had only a few years to live, though that could not be suspected in a world which dazzled with ideas. Within a few years Kate had taken some of these ideas to Washington, working indirectly on behalf on the newly declared Irish Free State, her American sojourn giving an authority to the final section of *Without My Cloak* in which Denis Considine hopelessly looks for his fugitive beloved in the half-lit late-nineteenth-century world of port-side New York, a section where Kate, like some maverick folk-song writer, seems to have trapped all the acumen of an archetypal experience.

But before Washington Kate worked briefly on the *Manchester Guardian*, living in Manchester, and taught two terms at a London school. An incident there prepares us for the heroine of *Mary Lavelle* (1936). Kate's beauty and graciousness made such an impact on the girls she was teaching that a mother traipsed to the convent to see what was astir, to be met at the door by a nun who declared, 'Well the fact is the beloved is very beautiful.' 1922–3 Kate was in another country, Spain. Which was to be the love of her life, a country from which she was barred from 1937 to 1957 for expressed Republican sympathies (*Farewell Spain*, 1937). In Bilbao in the rainy winter of 1922–3 Kate was acquainted with an Englishman who when she encountered him years later could only disdainfully recall the mud. Kate loved the mud for it reminded her of Ireland. In the Middle Ages there was constant commercial traffic between Spain and the West Coast of Ireland. A dark people on the West Coast of Ireland, the street names of certain Irish towns – in Galway there are names like Madeira Street, Velasquez de Palmeira Boulevard – bear witness to this.

In 1922 Ireland had a new link with Spain. It exported governesses. Kate joined the misses, the 'legions of the lost ones, the cohorts of the damned', the women who spoke English imperfectly and bided their time in cafés, hoping for the consummation of marriage. In *Mary Lavelle* there is a gesture of renunciation of Ireland, less publicized than Joyce's, but, for me, more tender, more universal. A young, already betrothed, Irish governess, naked in the night after seducing a young married Spaniard, realizes she has sold 'the orthodox code of her life', she has burnt her boats. 'She would answer it, taking the consequences.' Like Agnes in *The Ante-Room*, Clare in *As Music and Splendour*, Ana in *That Lady*. She accepts the lifelong totality of a single choice. In a way the night of lost virginity in *Mary Lavelle* dawns into the burning days under the Guadarramas in *That Lady*; Ana, older than Mary, still carries the struggle ensuing from the same choice. She knows she must let the consequences of her choice run their full gamut before she can connect again with her immortal soul. The landscape of Castile itself, eternal, unyielding, becomes a foil to the consternation within her. Mary in *Mary Lavelle* visits Castile for the first time and perceives it as 'meeting place of Moor and monk', a land where the miracles of the New Testament could comfortably have taken place. Her persona as it is developed in the character of Ana de Mendoza is destined to seek the miracle of salvation here in spite of an adulterous affair she regards as a mortal sin.

In 1923 Kate married a young Dutch journalist in a registry office, cohabiting with him in a confined space in Belsize Park; often, Kate would recollect, the two would stroll in state into London, pretending it was for exercise, whereas in fact the real reason for these promenades was lack of money. The marriage lasted a year. *Distinguished Villa*, Kate's first play, produced in 1926, a study of the middle classes of Brixton, was very nearly a tremendous success but its run was ended by the General Strike. The British papers in 1932 were describing a remarkably comely Irish woman, whom many thought was just over from Limerick, going to collect the Hawthornden Prize. As long as English was so beautifully used by Irish people, one paper gushed, Ireland and England could never really be enemies. Kate's age was given as either thirty or thirty-one. In fact Kate's first novel, *Without My Cloak*, was published on her thirty-fourth birthday in December 1931. Kate's second two novels, *The Ante-Room* and *Mary Lavelle*, are each a giddy leap ahead of the last. The first wavering of quality is her fourth novel, *Pray for the Wanderer* (1938). But there is a remark that seems to have gathered force with the development of Kate's life. The hero, an expatriate Irish writer, briefly home on a visit to a grey, Southern, riverside city, reflects that 'a life of absence predicates a life of absence'.

Kate chose England for the war. During the war she published *The Land of Spices* and *The Last of Summer* (1943). Among the flying bombs she wrote her most structured novel, a novel which reveals itself like the panels of a painting, *That Lady*. Amid the dramatic consternation of her time everything in the novel impels towards the inner life of Ana de Mendoza. She is a woman of middle age, one-eyed, a little ridiculous looking, but, to those who are intimate with her, magnetically sensual and emotionally calming. The post-war reading public loved her and *That Lady* sold more than half a million copies in its first few years of publication. The book was filmed. 'I went to see it one afternoon,' Kate says, 'and there were lots of little boys in the cinema. They were booing and whistling and, of course, were absolutely right. I agreed with them and left the cinema.'

On the proceeds from the book, film version, stage version, Kate moved to Ireland; she was possessed by the old Celtic dream that one should die in Ireland; for her prospective burial she picked out a hill overlooking a beach near Roundstone. She purchased a house in Roundstone, one occasionally plagued by rats whom some local shop proprietors muttered were the Tuatha De Danann in disguise. But in spite of the magic of white beaches and mystic rats, *The Flower of May* (1953) shows a diminishing of tension. Her next and last novel, *As Music and Splendour* (1958), was not a success and though marred by languor it is iridescently memorable for its depiction of 'complicated dusts and civilizations' and of lesbian love. Clare, a young Irish opera singer in Rome at the end of the last century, brings a Catholic sense of fidelity to a lesbian relationship only to be shattered to find that others are not inured to the same sense of fidelity even in something as extreme and as, to her, soul-risking as lesbian love. The end of Kate O'Brien's life in fiction is Clare walking into an uncertain and lonely life. A sense of sin, chosen and clung to, has a say in the last paragraph of *As Music and Splendour*.

Having sold her house in Roundstone in 1961 Kate moved to Boughton, near Faversham in Kent, where she secured a little house. In *The Ante-Room* an English doctor, Sir Godfrey Bartlett-Crowe, who realizes that Dublin has at least a few good wine cellars in its favour, ventures into 'the murderous and stormy South' to be taken aback by the elegance of the Mulqueen family. Sir Godfrey would have been equally surpised to find a member of such a family living in the south-east corner of England in the

1960s. Kate's family was always haunted by the fear of declining fortunes. Aunt Hickey, of Mespil Road, Dublin, used to shopping in Switzers, on bankruptcy trained her parrot to say 'Damn Switzers' on which she would approve him, 'Good boy, Sam.'

I don't know what Kate's attitude to her new relative obscurity was. Her books were following one another out of print. But she maintained a distinguished and acerbic poise in her column in the *Irish Times*. In *English Diaries and Journals* she quoted Katherine Mansfield: 'And when I say "I fear" don't let it disturb you, dearest heart. We all fear when we are in waiting rooms. Yet we must pass beyond them, and if the other can keep calm, it is all the help we can give each other.' One is reminded of the stolid devotion of Bernardina to Ana at the end, and of Ana's final isolation, from the world of glamour she was accustomed to, from the world of company, her last and only contact being her daughter. One is reminded of the anguish of Kate's last months in a hospital ward, deprived of her classical music and her Radio Four quiz programmes, forced to listen to the clatter of Radio One and Two. Two weeks after having a leg amputated she died. On her gravestone in Faversham cemetery is a simple epitaph from a childhood hymn of Kate's: 'Pray for the Wanderer.' In *The Flower of May* is a paragraph that compels with relevance.

Fanny looked about the beautiful wide table, at the gleaming glass and heavy silver, at the Sèvres plates and dishes; she smelt and appraised the radiant fruits; she tasted her golden wine and looked with attention at the many splendid faces, ageing and young and very young, about her in the gentle lamplight. 'It is a lovely scene,' she thought, 'all this civilisation, generosity and peace; all this blind, easy grace, this taking for granted of perfection in small things; all these radiant eyes, all this well-mannered affection, all this assurance, this polish, physical and even mental. But I belong to another place. I have dallied, I have dawdled. None of this is either mine or what I want. Mother, I am coming home.'

Kate never finally got home or wanted to go home.

New Year 1969 Kate put these words in the *Irish Times*. 'Private life remains – and cannot be taken away, except by death. Though, as Marvell reminded us very truly, "The grave's a fine and private place."'' *That Lady*, her most commercially successful novel, is about private life, Ana de Mendoza's attempt to preserve private emotions against the carnivorous demands of her society and her time, and her attempt to preserve a knowledge of her soul against a passionate and very physical love affair. In *Teresa of Avila* (1951) Kate makes reference to a follower of Teresa who, after her death, left his Carmelite order and spent the rest of his life wandering as a tramp in North Africa. Ana de Mendoza is another such character. Her life a side-show of history. She stumbled out of 'The Letters of Saint Teresa' for Kate, Teresa having had a run-in with the princess. It is not the organization of historical events and characters, the arabesque of place-names that finally impresses, but the imaginative totality Kate brings to the emotional life of Ana de Mendoza. Philip is the other character that is wholly palpable, but despite his tangibility he is a wraith-like character; time, the Nazis, what you will. Ana de Mendoza realizes that once an action has begun – her affair – she must see it through against all other principles, and when it has run its course she can connect again with the journey of her salvation. Not before. Kate O'Brien's theme can be summed up in two words: 'Nunc Dimittis'. The life of experience chosen and lived to the point you can say 'Now I've lived; now experience has come to its logical conclusion and now I can tend again to the acreage of spiritual life within me and that alone.'

Ana de Mendoza is a woman pitted against a time of manifold danger and much chaos; her reservoir of emotions is filled by the world her emotions must fight against; her triumph, and the book's, is that her persona transcends its time, its enemies, and time itself with the magnitude of its sensitivity and the depths of its intuitions. Ana is a child of any time when the idea of individuality is attacked, when inner life is under fire, when individuals must square up to the notions of their monomaniac kings. Ana's struggle against the king is, apart from anything else, a wonderful story; the king's final punishment a birth for her and a revelation for the reader. And the fact that Ana

happens to be a sixteenth-century Spanish princes points Kate in
the direction of lines by Marina Tsvetayeva:

> Back to the land of Dreams and Loneliness –
> Where we – are Majesties, and Highnesses.

Israel

The most memorable Christmas I've had actually began in October. In October 1982, after the invasion of Lebanon and after the massacre at Sabra and Chatila, I spent some weeks in Israel.

Around the Lebanese border soldiers on foot constantly milled on the roads, a kind of treadmill of weary soldiery.

The Mediterranean sun was still suitable for tourist brochures. There were the lonely Australian voices by the sea.

I was staying mainly in Jerusalem. The sounds of the West Bank were occasional, muffled, but insistent at night. On the Sabbath a run-down bus took me to Bethlehem.

The landscape threw together West Belfast and Connemara. Stony hills, decaying housing. I crossed a square. Goats picnicked on scraps. Confectionery dazzled on tables, green of pistachio, cream of yogurt, buff of nougat, dark of hazlenuts and almonds, the intensity of saffron. In cafés, under pictures of Tracy Ullman, men sipped Turkish coffees, eyes suspiciously lifting towards you. The Star of David, white against blue, flying high, determined ownership of the square. There weren't many tourists in sight that day and a few Scandinavian women and myself had the Church of the Nativity to ourselves. There were Scandinavian prayers at the site of the Nativity.

My journey to Bethlehem on an October afternoon reminded me of the way Boris Pasternak, in his poem 'Christmas Star', translated the experience of the Nativity to Russia and how Andrei Tarkovsky, in his film *Andrei Rublev*, transferred the crucifixion to a snowy Russian hill. In London now they say that Christ has come back and is a social worker in the Deptford area. Posters to that effect have gone up on poles around the city.

Bethlehem put me in mind of childhood, childhood beyond violence, things of childhood safe from violence, from the Massacre of the Innocents. Bethlehem put me in mind of a convent crib in Ballinasloe, its cloistered dark, the pink Cellophane on the lantern, the pungent and high tang of straw in the air, the whispered prayers of a rustic nun. In a country where the war tanks rapidly overtook the camel riders in the blanched deserts there was still contact with the electricity of this famed birth.

You move away from a place, you take some of its electricity with you. At Christmas, friends, not seen for a long time, turned up from many parts of the world. Christmas Eve we went to the midnight service at St James's, Piccadilly. A girl in a white blouse and long black crêpe dress gave us a few bars of oboe music to evoke the angels.

In the following two years there have been births – two babies – and deaths for those of our small group. But that night I felt the meaning of Christmas had changed for me by my having participated, briefly, in a landscape which was rocky, almost despairing, but from which, for a moment, you could hear the chorus of seraphims above houses on which the graffiti were like bullet wounds.

1987

Norway

Last November, tired of London, I decided to purchase a ticket out of it. Instead of going south I headed in the direction of the North Pole.

On 14 November I took an afternoon flight to Oslo, arriving there in pitch, freezing black. I didn't know a soul in this city. Outside the main railway station boys and girls in mammoth wellingtons swept up leaves. I was reminded of a favourite line from Tennessee Williams. 'The cities swept about me like dead leaves, leaves that were brightly coloured but torn away from the branches.' Having heard of the astronomical prices in this country I'd brought a youth hostel card with me. I stayed that night in a youth hostel outside Oslo. Just after I'd fallen asleep about midnight the window of my room opened from the outside and five Moroccan youths with rucksacks entered. They arranged sleeping bags around the room. Just before seven in the morning they collected their belongings and got out, in an orderly file, through the same window. A week later Norway was under oblivionizing snow.

In one of the stories of mine I like best an Irish tinker woman of middle age escapes with her new husband, to the south, just after the war. 'They passed war ruins and posters showing brazen women. They weaved through towns where summer lingered in February and rode hills where spring came like an onlooker, gazing at them with eyes of cherry blossom. They lingered on a mound of earth as they caught sight of the blue, blue sea.' Like her I perpetually feel the need to escape through travel. I beg for, humiliate myself for the money to go, eke it out

of nearly empty cupboards. But my escapes, as in the case of
Norway, are not always to the 'blue, blue sea'.

Where I live now in Catford my two tiny rooms are crammed
with postcards from foreign places. There has been a mass
exodus of people from my life but the postcards are still there,
postcards of Chartres, of Nice, of Venice, evidence of former
escapes.

The memoirs of
Nadezhda Mandelstam

In George's Bar, Iowa City, autumn 1981, I encountered a Polish poet who had been studying medicine in Leningrad in March 1953 when Stalin died. George's Bar was a stopping point for long-distance truck drivers, funereal red and purple lights in the window. In the covert darkness of this place she told me how on the day of Stalin's death the girls in her dormitory wept. A few days later when they were told to be joyful and roar with laughter they were joyful and roared with laughter. Her story reminded me of a bizarre anecdote in *Hope Abandoned*, the second book of memoirs by Nadia Mandelstam, widow of the murdered Russian poet Osip Mandelstam.

In the middle of the night, shortly before Stalin's death, she was woken and brought to a special meeting at the teacher training college where she lectured in languages, women in crêpe de Chine dresses gathered there, despite the late hour, one woman with a silver fox fur draped over her shoulder in the manner of Russian film actresses. Nadia was informed that in her classes she'd been setting the English gerund at war with the old infinitive, which indicated that she felt there was enmity between Soviet fathers and sons. She was told to pack and leave. Before she left news came of Stalin's death. As she was walking out of the door she saw a Jewish couple from the mathematics department, who had been similarly dismissed, dancing together in the courtyard, gone mad. Stalin's death had come too late for them.

For twenty years after Mandelstam was finally taken away on 1 May 1938 Nadia Mandelstam kept the words of most of his poems in her memory. Sequences of his poems were buried all

45

over Russia and when they turned up in the Khrushchev era some of the poems were found to have people like Brigitte Bardot as their subject matter, which was slightly odd! Memory had proved a safer place. Mandelstam had been hounded by Stalin because of a derogatory poem he'd written about him: 'The huge laughing cockroaches of his top lip,/the glitter of his boot-rims.' In the late 1950s, despite Mandelstam's rehabilitation, Nadia Mandelstam was denied permission to live in Moscow and in Pskov, 430 miles from Moscow, started into her memoirs which, ironically, she could not have done in a writers' apartment block in Moscow where she would have been under constant and mendacious surveillance. The results were *Hope Against Hope* and *Hope Abandoned*, published abroad in 1970 and 1972.

Hope Against Hope reads like the best detective novel ever written, Stalin's pursuit of Mandelstam – the years of exile for Mandelstam and his wife, the lulls in persecution, the apparent relaxations of mood at the Kremlin, the times Osip and Nadia Mandelstam had to beg on the side of the road for survival, the times they sauntered around Moscow and Leningrad, only able to get into these cities for hours when they could get sustenance from people like the poetess Anna Akhmatova, Mandelstam's final disappearance after he'd been seduced away with his wife on a kind of writer's honeymoon at a writers' rest home, the reconstructed journey towards death, by train, by barge, by boat, to a zenith where people chopped off their toes because they were so frozen with cold.

Hope Abandoned is a more philosophical work, a mad, fulminating, funny, affectionate book, the fatter of the two. Everywhere in its pages, through description of horror – a time when children of party officials in a rural district beat up and robbed travellers and then gouged out their eyes so they, the assailants, would not be later identified – through description of illustrious contemporaries like the poetess Marina Tsvetayeva – 'I know of no fate more terrible than Marina Tsvetayeva's' – the devotion of Nadia's love for Osip shines through. 'He lived with us always and never left us.'

Whether in a dissertation on the use of red in Rembrandt's *The*

Prodigal Son or in a story about a shoemaker, once taken away and beaten to the point of death by the authorities, who made shoes of many colours, from bits and pieces, for Nadia in Tashkent during the war, these books are enthralling.

Nadia Mandelstam lived on in an apartment in south-west Moscow until December 1980, probably the twentieth-century's greatest survivor. At one point in *Hope Abandoned* she talks about the difference between people who think that God is in their head, that they are God, and people who let God, truth, shine through them. The first state, I often think, describing Stalin and his followers, is as relevant to psychiatrists I meet and journalists I read in contemporary London, who apparently think that truth is cauterized in their heads, that they are God, that there is nothing beyond the intellect. What lies beyond the intellect Nadia Mandelstam puts like this: 'All that really matters is the inner light. This, and only this, is important.'

Galicia

The proprietor of the last old bar on Avienda de Areal in Vigo, which is otherwise lined by discothèques, thronged by young people in the glitter of their evening clothes, was going there. He was shutting shop on 24 and 25 July to be there. The tap over the basin dripped as he told me this, his poodle took little irascible snipes at my ankles. Above the counter was a picture of a line of soldiers saluting the crucified Christ. I went there for the festivities to mark St James's Day on 25 July and discovered the wider area of Galicia, the north-western region of Spain, which Santiago de Compostela represents.

It had always been a rumour for me; a place of hidden-away, untouched beauty. Now it manifested itself after a trip by bus and train from Lisbon. There are four provinces in Galicia: Pontevra, Orense, Lugo and A Coruna to the very north-west where Santiago de Compostela is situated and where I spent most time while there. The province of Lugo to the north-east offers similiar ancientness, towns which have huge annual horse fairs dating back much further than the Ballinasloe Horse Fair.

There was someone in Santiago who'd walked there from Zurich, another person who'd walked there from Marseille. Once it was Christendom's biggest pull. The body of St James, the apostle who'd introduced Christianity to Spain, was brought in by boat to Padron in Galicia after he'd been martyred in Palestine. The mooring stone is still in Padron. I walked down by the river looking for it and met a woman leading sheep. One monument by the river had washing attached to it. It could not have been that. Eventually I found it in a church. A woman

48

snipping carnations threw open doors under the altar to show it to me.

St James's body was lost for a few centuries and then, in the ninth century, the light of a star indicated it in a field. Thus Campus Stellae. The jumble of streets which is the centre of Santiago de Compostela. The popularity of St James's bones caught on. One of his hands got to Reading and it was from England in the Middle Ages that some of the most fervent pilgrims came. Chaucer's Wife of Bath was one. The Way of St James begins on the Spanish side of the Pyrenees. It is 700 kilometres long. Walking twenty-five kilometres a day it takes about a month to walk. I met an Englishman who'd cycled there. It had taken him nine days from the Pyrenees. He'd started cycling at Bordeaux. An English ballad of the Middle Ages suggested conditions on the pilgrim boat to Bordeaux:

> A man were as good to be dead
> As smell thereof the stink.

On the early afternoon of 23 July Santiago was quiet as a mortuary. Silence was broken by a Lembranza of Vigo. A young man in a black, wide-brimmed, papal-type hat, bearing a gold banner with an emblem of a green tree in its centre, led the parade from the gardens of Santa Susana, of other young men in all types of hats, jockey-type hats, tea-cosies of hats, Napoleon-type hats, and young women in lace headdresses and patterned scarves. The music of tambourines, drums and three- or four-pronged bagpipes had to compete with the hymn of Tombolael Cubo being sung by another young man in his stand in the nearby fair, among the prizes of white furry cats and dolls stretching out immobilized arms.

The festivities reached a climax on the night of 24 July when the Romanesque and baroque front of the cathedral became a living tableau of fireworks, the almost clownish figures of Master Mateo standing out against the illuminations: bunting, haystacks of fireworks in the sky over Santiago.

I had stayed on Calle del Franco which leads from the gardens of Santa Susana to Plaza del Obradoiro, the cathedral square.

There was no sleep to be had while there. The street outside was an inferno at night, a river of students in black cloaks bleating on bagpipes with even the odd waiter in restaurants taking time off to bleat on a bagpipe in the restaurant. If you're someone who needs sleep it's better to go to Santiago at another time.

In Santiago is the museum of the Galician people and there you can see models of the Galician countryside, a countryside liberally impregnated with *horreos* – granaries on stilts – with tall, strange crosses, crosses which you even see on cakes, especially the *tarta flamendra*. This is a land of the Celts of course. According to *Leabhar Gabhála*, the Book of Invasions, it was from the tower of Corunna that Ireland was first sighted by a Celt – a dark blob on the sea. The same fellow was killed in Ireland and subsequently, according to the book, Ireland was invaded by Spanish magicians. James Fitzgerald docked in Galicia during one of his expeditions from Lisbon to Ireland, the Breton captain making off with his boat! Galicia implodes with estuaries. The wonder of the countryside is that you don't have to scurry off to museums and churches. Every road you walk down has its own church, a saint over the entrance with rouge peeling from the saintly, medieval cheeks.

From the utterly ugly bus station in Corunna you can take buses to the loveliest of places, seaside resorts which look like film-sets of late 1950s resorts in Greece, one or two pensions in them maybe, the beginnings of a discothèque. I escaped Santiago to visit some of these resorts: Cayon, Baldayo, Malpica, Lage, all on the north coast, beaches of absolute white with an ice-cream glitter, forests of pine tumbling down on to them, the Atlantic never less than dramatic. From the north coast I headed to Cape Finisterre on the north-west coast. That had been the conclusion of the medieval pilgrimage. It was the last post on earth. Pilgrims came here to contemplate life's infinities. In sublime July weather the coast around Finisterre looked like a cross between West Mayo and northern California. There was nothing threatening to be seen or felt here. The weather kept up, giving a stained-glass quality to the visuals on the rest of my journey down the coast, to a woman in black, black headdress, sauntering on to a bus, to the beaches which had changed, now azure and pacific, to Cape Finisterre which persisted behind for miles, ruling this coast until suddenly you were in another province, Pontevedra, which was lusher, more populated and where instead of crosses there were palm trees and high-rise buildings.

From Las Sinas beach at Villaneuva de Arosa with its cavalcade of palm trees I looked across the bay, strewn with fishing platforms, to the hills of A Coruna which were quietly being snuffed out by a lilac evening.

There are things I'll never forget about this trip to Galicia; the bar by the sea in Malpica where the proprietor had stuck newspaper photographs of twentieth-century history all over the walls with Sellotape, especially photographs of the Spanish Civil War, but also ones from the concentration camps; the country people in Plaza del Obradoiro on 24 July, playing accordions, wild flowers in the breast pockets of old suits, a woman singing a verse, then a man answering her with a verse, then the woman singing again, all the time the sun going down, a secretive red on the medieval stones of the square.

One drawback: outside Santiago there are few places to stay. One night in a remote town I was directed to a café which was part of the funeral parlour (Funeraria San José) for accommodation!

I could not talk about Galicia without mentioning Ribero wine, a sharp white wine. There is often a ceremony in getting it, the attendant fetching it in a jug from a barrel and then pouring it from the jug into a little bowl. As the sign in the window of a little Lincoln-green pub in Padron said, a pub whose door was shut and where I had to knock to get in: 'Hermano, bebe que la vida es breve.' 'Comrade, have a drink because life is short.' At ten pence a go who wouldn't.

An interview with Van Morrison

'I'm just channelling. That's what I do. I say it's a collective unconscious. That's what I prefer to call it. I'm channelling these ideas that are coming through me from wherever they are I don't know. I myself am not actually saying anything either way. I just get ideas coming through. It might be a line. A bit of a melody. I develop these things that come through the subconscious mind and put shapes on them and they become songs. And basically that's what I do. I haven't a clue what that's about myself, am trying to find out. I'm just putting down what I get and recording it.'

Van Morrison's latest album, *Poetic Champions Compose*, speaks of risk, trust, entering the sun, the mystery, dancing. I'd asked him if he thought that in these grim times it might have a counter-active effect for the good.

We met in the lounge of the Shepherd's Bush Hilton. Only time I'd been in the Hilton, I told him, had been in Cairo where you could get breakfast for fifty pence.

He was a stocky figure in dark clothes. Only bright thing about his apparel was the magazine he was carrying, which he looked at when I sat down. Last person to do that to me was a member of the Gurdjieff-Ouspensky movement. I interpreted it as coming from decades of suspicion of interviewers. But it was, thankfully, a brief gesture on his part. He asked me what my angle was. I said I had none. He said that boded badly. There'd been a good interview on Radio Derry, he said.

From *Astral Weeks* to *Poetic Champions Compose* Van Morrison has retained a priestly integrity. He's been an artist in the music

world who always seems to write from his inner life. I asked him
how he'd retained and protected that inner space.

'You see there's two things happening, right. One thing – A –
is the work itself. Basically. Writing the songs. Putting shapes on
the songs. Putting down ideas for arrangements. How they
should be done. Going into the studios. Developing the ideas.
Developing the lines. Rewriting them. All this kind of thing.
That's one thing. That process is separate from the other process
which would be the B part of it. The part you're going out with,
what you have to encounter business people with. You have to
deal with the level they're operating on to sell this piece of what
they call product. A and B are completely different and very,
very much apart from one another and that's just the way it is.'

But some people mix them up?

'Exactly. What happened to me, I was early on forced into the
role as producer. This role as producer put me in that situation
where I was actually producing records and delivering the
masters. In other words there was no middleman in between.
That's put me more in the position where I'm doing what I want
to do. But then when it comes to the point of selling what I've
done it puts me in the other position where I have to deal with a
lot more people, what they think and what they believe, which is
basically the music business. I see them as being separate things.
One's a creative process. The other's a selling process. You're
dealing with entirely different things. The main reason that I had
control is that I'm a producer. Even if I hire another producer I'm
still the producer. The wave I came in on, that was a breakthrough because before that you had producers and A&R men
and they were usually calling the shots. The wave I came in on,
that was a breakthrough for people getting control of their work.'

But there'd obviously been very serious encroachment on him
as an artist and as a human being at times I suggested.

'Also some of that encroachment taught me lessons as well.
This is what you have to understand as well. Because you have to
be able to deal in all angles. If you're just dealing, say, on the
creative level and not bothered about how things operate when

you're dealing with hardcore facts of the business world then you're sort of walking into walls. You have to be aware of that as well. What you're in is a tough business and you have to be very aware. The way I put it: I don't suffer fools gladly.'

Was that always the way?

'No that's not always been the way. To get where I am I've had to fight. It's still a fight. It's still a struggle. It's still a fight. I mean I'm not playing same game I played twenty years ago. My particular stance at this time is that I've gone through the rock and roll stars . . . I've been a star I don't know how many times. I was a teenage star. So I went through being a teenage star. Then I went through being a twenty-year-old star. Then a singer–song-writer star. I went through that one. I found out what that was all about. I learnt my lessons and I took my blows. By the time I was twenty-seven I'd done that one. I'd gone through my second phase of being a rock star. That's what they called it in those days. But I didn't call it that. I'd already wrapped that up by the time I was twenty-eight. I started a whole new career. When I came back into the music business I started a whole new phase because I was no longer that person. I'd done that and I'd worked that out. For the past twelve years or so I've only been in it part of the time. I'm only in the music business part-time now. I finished with that whole thing then. I've run the gamut, I took the blows. I realized I've lived that out and I didn't have to do it any more.'

I said that Sartre objected to people hiding behind categories of painters, musicians, writers: their work was them and otherwise they were unlabelled human beings. Van Morrison said that was it exactly.

I asked him about the sense of light and dark in his work, like the Irish weather, the fight between the two.

'That came from having to do things . . . A lot of people say to me, well you're really lucky. I'm not lucky. At certain times I had to do certain things and that's really the way it was. I didn't have a choice. It was either A or B. I did the one thing that happened to get me through. It wasn't a matter of sitting up in an ivory tower at the time and saying, I wonder whether I want to do A or B or

C. In the sixties you didn't have a choice. You were either in the van on the M1 going up and down the M1 doing gigs or doing nothing. When the singer–song-writer thing first appeared there wasn't a choice. You had to do that a certain way and the people that were in charge, they did things a certain way. If you wanted that you had to compromise. There was a lot of compromise and a lot of hard graft I had to do. But it got me to a point where I did have a choice.'

Sometimes in his obsession with childhood the images are amorphous – rain, sun, light; sometimes it comes up close, like black and white images in the Bill Douglas film trilogy: '. . . marching with soldier boy behind. He's much older now with hat on, drinking wine.' '. . . the kids out in the street, collecting bottle tops, gone for cigarettes and matches in the shops.' '. . . the train from Dublin up to Sandy Row, throwing pennies at the bridges down below, in the rain, hail, sleet and snow.' '. . . wee Alfie at the Castle picture house on the Castlereagh Road.' '. . . whistling on the corner next door where he kept John Mack Brown's horse.'

Did he find that he, like a lot of Irish people who left Ireland, had to block out the specifics of his early life at times?

'I didn't really have a choice about any of it until I was like twenty-eight. Before that it was either put up or shut up. It was a struggle financially. I didn't even start making money until I was twenty-eight. For me that was a time I couldn't even consider looking at biography. All I did from the time I was like eighteen to twenty-seven was work. I worked my way from Belfast to New York and didn't even know I was there because it was work.'

I get the impression he goes back to Ireland much more now.

'You see there's all different levels to this. There's the personal level. Then there's the career level. I don't get into the personal level in a situation like an interview. It's mine. All I discuss in interviews, it's business, it's promotion for a record or something. Other than that I'm not available for anything else.'

Yes, but in some of his recent work, in a fairly recent song like 'Sense of Wonder', Ireland is much more up front: '. . . the man who played the saw outside the City Hall', ' "O Solo Mio" by McGinsey'.

(Just then someone began banging what I thought might have been Beethoven's 'Für Elise' on the nearby piano.)

'I was actually reading a Michael Bentine book. It kept saying something about "sense of wonder". I picked up another book or something . . . something about "sense of wonder". So that went into the subconscious. I was sitting down one day and playing the guitar. "Sense of wonder . . . sense of wonder." That's my process. I remembered something about Ballystockart. I went there. That developed into a song. That's not me personally. Truman Capote called it faction. Part fact. Part fiction. You're painting on things. Part of it's fact. Part of it's fiction. That's really what I'm doing. I have to see what I'm doing in retrospect. Then I edit it. I shape it.'

Van Morrison says about 'A Sense of Wonder' that he 'ties it in with nature in Ireland'. It's about 'the vibration of nature in Ireland'. He says about what I considered his most seminal recent song, 'In the garden', from *No Guru, No Method, No Teacher* that it's about 'Christianity and nature combined'. On the album *Common One* he made a literary nature pilgrimage, to Coole Park.

'That was actually from a poem I wrote. That actual part of that song. I wrote a poem and put part of the poem in that song at that place. That's what that was. I was going to do that poem on its own and instead of doing that I put it in that part of the song. I don't even know if it was connected myself.'

On the subject of Yeats I asked him about similarities between his songs and Yeats's poems, in my mind less the mysticism than the way romanticism, allure comes to Cypress Avenue, the Castlereagh Road.

'Don't really know. You see I got that idea from someone else. It didn't really put me on the right track. Somebody wrote an article about me a while back. They were trying to say there were similarities between my songs and Yeats's poems. At the time it seemed like, you know, a good idea. Through further exploration I discovered it's not my lineage. It is in a certain way my lineage. It's a bit sort of academic. Put it that way. Even though I can get academic. My lineage would be more A.E. [George Russell]. That's more my lineage. That sort of mysticism as opposed to Yeats's mysticism.'

At one point, referring indirectly to Blake, I said I preferred to use the word religious rather than mystic.

'The thing is you have to use mysticism if you're talking on theological terms so you've got a reference point. If you say religious you could mean anything. I use mytic that way.'

His newest songs talk of the necessity of openness. Can the vulnerability of openness not be extremely dangerous? I asked him.

'I never see it that way. Open to something that's dangerous? I don't see it like that. I see it the other way. If you're closed that's more dangerous. That's dangerous, being closed.'

Yes, but he'd said he'd learnt to protect his openness.

'Not the actual creativity part. I'm talking about that other part of it which is, you know . . . I mean if you're in the Holiday Inn in the middle of nowhere on a tour on an off Sunday night or something and you're fed up you can't walk off the tour. It doesn't protect you from that. I'm talking about the openness of the creativity. The other thing I relate to, you're in a boxing ring the rest of the time. The creativity is open enough. But it's when you go out there you're out in the jungle, it's different. It's not about creativity, it's not about openness. You have to protect yourself just like you're in the ring. You've got to have gloves on there. It's a different situation.'

I talked about people I'd known who'd, quoting a recent phrase of Van Morrison himself which echoed Blake, 'drunk of the fountains of innocence' and were destroyed.

'There again you see it's poems of innocence *and* experience. That's what I was talking about before. The reason I'm able to do that is that I've been able to work through that and taken the blows. It's songs of innocence *and* experience if you read the lyrics. To sing about innocence you need the experience. That's what it is. To be totally, completely innocent is absolutely useless and will get you absolutely nowhere. They will cave you in.'

I told him I'd intended to record this conversation over a tape of *Cabaret*. (The piano was banging louder than ever.) He didn't seem to find that funny. I asked him if he thought he'd stay in London. He said he didn't know.

Then I asked him what his favourite place in Ireland was.

At first he seemed either unwilling or unable to answer. Then he said: 'East Belfast.'

1988

Catford

It was Bert who wove my life into secret Catford. Bert is a retired photographer who lives up the road from me in a grove of early-nineteenth-century houses off the South Circular. I first saw my potential flat in May 1982, forget-me-nots running up to the french windows. After years of peregrination from room to room in London I hoped it would be my flat. As it turned out I was lucky and on a dank day that autumn I carried my belongings through those french windows. Outside, in the mornings, a ninety-year-old woman would merrily sweep leaves, string upon string of jewels around her neck. My landlady would scurry down the steps in black, off to conduct an atheist funeral. She is a kind of atheist prelate. But the road beyond the grove seemed grey and drab and depleted of life save for the oddity of a woman crossing it in wartime padded shoulders, save for the shop at the corner where two old ladies in blue overalls would preside in the semi-dark behind wartime corsets, waiting for customers to enter this oblique scene. My cat, Eamon, started visiting Bert and I followed him. On my first visit Bert showed me the Rye jug which was made for him on his birth, vines climbing the jug. I began going for walks with Bert. From the top of Blythe Hill behind the grove he pointed out One Tree Hill where Elizabeth I picnicked: in the same spot, with a wave of his hand, he indicated a Roman road where it was suddenly manifest on Blythe Hill against the dramatics of the sky, a road which leads from New Cross to Lewes. Cap on his head he led me to a point on Catford Hill where you can slip through a gap in the wall and immediately the scene is uplifting and you can take an idyllic walk by the river Ravensbourne to Bellingham. Long Meadow Walk it is called. Bert has lots of ancient books and in my presence he opened one on a page about Thomas Dermody. Thomas Dermody was an Irish poet who fought in the Napoleonic wars, lived in Perry Slough on the opposite side of the South Circular, and drank himself to death at an early age. The verses Lady Byron composed in his memory were her introduction to Lord Byron.

> Degraded genius! o'er the untimely grave
> In which the tumults of thy breast were stilled.

On my bicycle I cycled to Dermody's stately tomb in the grounds of St Mary's in Lewisham. The bicycle became of paramount importance in Catford and its environs. On it I made a few trips to a travellers' encampment on the outskirts of Catford. In one of the caravans I was shown books of recent wedding photographs, matchstick barrel-caravans. A travelling lady told me how she'd won a beauty competition at the Puck Fair in Killorglin in 1955. Many of the children were born in England but they make frequent visits to Ireland, for the erection of a headstone on a grandmother's grave for instance, and they have pony races on disused patches of motorway beyond Woolwich. One little boy sang a Joe Dolan song for me, 'Julie', in such a way that it sounded like a ballad from the Napoleonic wars.

History seemed to come into everything. The barber at the top of Stanstead Road who has recently retired would talk as he cut your hair of his apprentice days in a barber's shop by the sea in Ramsgate. A boy clipping the whiskers of old men. Occasionally a punk girl entered while he reminisced. No, she had to come back on Saturday. His Polish partner was the one who cut the hair of punk girls. The Horniman Museum with its esoteric exhibitions, its flotsam of stuffed chimpanzees, has a patch of ground opposite which is still considered scourged, once the burial ground for plague victims.

To free myself of history I cycle through the flocks of gulls, of starlings in Ladywell Fields.

Talk in Catford can be savage and subterranean. The effigy of a black cat over the entrance to Catford shopping centre distracts you from the fact that Catford is called after a medieval burgher, John de Cateforde. A grey place, the old will always lament the beauty of buildings like the Eros or Gaumont cinemas long turned into office blocks. Anecdote abounds in the streets. As I passed a garage in Brockley once an old lady told me that when she was a child it was a slaughterhouse called Wellbeloved's and one day she saw a goose fly out if it and hide under a tram so that the tram was halted for the day because they couldn't get the goose out from underneath. Pubs are cited because they had Dick Turpin to visit – the Two Brewers on Catford Hill, the Brockley Jack. The Fox and Firkin where I drink scrumpy has a notice banning kissograms and makes its own beer in the back. On Mondays, Wednesdays and Saturdays the best talk goes to Catford Greyhound Stadium where, among the cries of 'Come on, Number Six', you hear the conversations of Irish travellers, the interchanges of modern highwaymen.

I followed Bert one night down Carholme Road to St George's Hall where we watched a performance of *A Letter to the General* by the St George's Players, the tableau of an old nun at the end who sits by lamplight, everybody in the mission safely departed with her help, and she waiting for the hordes. The audience that night was one of ladies in raffish-looking tea-cosy hats, of men in impeccable suits, very often tie pins on the sculpted curvature of their bellies. They are the kind of people who these days eagerly anticipate the opening of the Mander-Mitchenson theatrical collection at Place House in Beckenham Place Park, the most interesting collection of theatrical memorabilia in the country which has moved from the Mitchenson-Mander home in Sydenham. The applause at the end of the play was tumultuous, especially for the old nun. I'd seen *A Letter to the General* once before. In the town hall, Ballinasloe, County Galway, when I was a child.

It's for reasons like this that the grey of Catford and its outreaches has been illumined for me in the last six years, a carefully orchestrated ikon at the end of an amateur performance: on Deptford High Street, suddenly among the goatfish and the jackfish, as you pass on your bicycle, the face of an Irish travelling woman who won the beauty competition at the Puck Fair in Killorglin in 1955.

County Galway

I'd seen her get on a train in Galway city February of the previous year. A chiffon scarf wrapped around her plentiful white hair. A stout woman carrying a small bag. On the way to Dublin she piped a mysterious song: 'If you sit on a red hot poker it's the sign of an early spring.'

'Your memory must have gone with your looks,' she told a small, bespectacled man, standing over him, after having challenged him about some historical data. We never spoke but on the train from Holyhead, which had been greatly delayed, she sat near me, having been befriended by some Dublin boys who were emigrating. One of them had a penchant for 1950s songs and delivered 'My Wild Irish Rose', out in the aisle, a fashionable white polo neck on him, troubadour's thick quiff of blond hair on his forehead, in tribute to her. She and the boys left the train together at Euston. They were going to have bacon and eggs in a caff and then she was going to bring them to a nun in Wimbledon. She was on the deck of the boat that morning as it neared Dun Laoghaire, but as I got a lift to Galway that was the last I saw of her. First part of our town is Our Lady of Lourdes church in Creagh, standing up, alone there, like a tombstone. That is on the Roscommon side of the town. Then you cross a bridge and are in Galway. The mental hospital, which they started building in 1833, is on the Roscommon side of the town, but that doesn't save Galway from having the highest mental illness rate in Europe.

The smaller river which runs into the Suck had run dry – water-mint growing all over its basin, I found when I inspected it later on. This is where I used to meet my friends as a child. By the rivulet. A sanctuary. On the other side of it a carriageway, which circumvents the town, runs parallel to it now. The church near by had to be built in a marsh by decree of the local landlord but its steeple rose in spite higher than the spires of the Protestant church which sits on a hill. Cardinal Wiseman was borne on the shoulders of local people for its consecration and Napoleon III sent a vestment with the Bonaparte badge on it for the occasion. These were the stories we grew up with, stories that have stayed alongside stories of local people: the Czech women who ran a jewellery shop in town once. They had shunted and shifted all over Ireland, finding peace here for a while, then retired, lived in a house in Clontarf, Dublin, the eldest leaving me a tablecloth in her will, the youngest having died recently in an old people's home on the other side of Galway city among the rocks, the anarchic cabbage seed.

I'd visited Prague since last I'd been in the town. In the old Jewish cemetery there I'd thought of them and in the suburbs of Prague, under high-rise flats, a gypsy family on a bench waiting for a bus, I'd thought of the gypsies, the tinkers who'd encircled our town in winter when I was a child. They'd created a pattern for the lives of many of my contemporaries, a pattern of moving on, always moving on, nomads.

'Ah, Dagenham,' a woman had said in a buffet in Prague, 'Dagenham,' pulling at a hair on my naked arm. She'd been there once. I lived not far from Dagenham, near by a settlement of Irish travellers. I sometimes went there and heard stories about County Galway. How families of tinkers were turned away from cinemas there and spent the night instead reading comics by rural campfires. How tinkers got married there with rings made from teaspoons. Matchstick barrel-caravans were produced, possibly as memorials to County Galway. My town was quietly referred to, renowned and sacred because of its annual horse fair. In Gill's Hotel in Ballinasloe the local dignitaries gathered each year during the fair to celebrate the town, its achievements in the previous year. Now the town has meandered way outside its former tight nucleus, lizards of new streets, new avenues, a new type of child on their pavements, the streets, the avenues cutting into Garbally estate. The heir to the manor, much to the chagrin of his father, had once married a Cockney music hall artiste, Isabel Bilton. She was loved by all when she became lady of the manor and her legend lingered right up to my childhood in the 1950s. I think I was very lucky. Galway imploded with stories, many of them too intense ever to write down. Perhaps the best stories we carry with us, within us, never to be written down. But there was always a sense of making something from experience. In Naughton's pub in Galway city, as I entered, a young man on a bar stool belted out a song he might have made up himself.

> There's not enough work in this country,
> There's not enough land to go round.

Galway Arts Festival was on, at night the streets around the Claddagh jammed with young people drinking beer, wine, the odd guitarist among them, crouched on the ground, drawing his audience. On the walls by the canal the sexuality of Jesuit boys was impugned, the IRA praised. A giant puppet of Gulliver, which had recently taken part in the Dublin millennium parade, was outstretched on a beach near Salthill. By Claddagh Bridge were a newly sown wild cherry tree and Italian maple tree. They might have been sown, in this city of youth, for some of County Galway's defeated and exiled, the Czech lady who'd ended her days west of Galway city when in fact her home had been east of it.

For years when I got to Galway, Clifden, in the north-west of it, was the first place I headed to. Another garrison town like Ballinasloe to the very east of it. But this time I'd dallied in the town I was from, in Galway city. I've stayed with the same old lady for years in Clifden. She's become my great friend. In her mid seventies, much of the time on buses in Ireland, on her way to see Oliver Plunkett's head in Drogheda, making a pilgrimage to Lough Derg. You'll often see her between buses, at a bus stop, in a tracksuit. In Drogheda once at the opening of a disco the DJ asked her if he could put blue in her hair and dance with her. She was after a day's praying so why not? But the blue didn't come out for six months. One of her many stories. Like the story of how, in her négligé, she was attacked by a fox and her only fear was that her dead body would be found naked. A picture of Our Lady of Medugorje, the latest Lady, over the mantelpiece. 'I could have filled the field with all the boyfriends I had.' The stories continued into the night. She was married twice but both her husbands are long dead. Her children live in Galway city. One of her sons, his wife and two adopted children went to London the previous Christmas, intending to stay, but returned after a brief sojourn to poverty in Galway. 'The moment we cease to hold each other, the moment we break faith with one another, the sea engulfs us and the light goes out,' James Baldwin wrote somewhere. There may be few jobs in Galway city but there is an enfolding, a mantling sense of community.

In Galway city I'd seen a former heroin-addict friend dance in an old church converted into an arts centre. It might have been a dance from a Yeats play. *The Herne's Egg*, for instance. He was alone there in the centre of the floor.

> The real world, the otherworld, is behind us and beyond us, out of our ken, and all we are aware of is the vague shadow of reality flickering in the things we see.

One of the last lines of the Ballinasloe poet Eoghan O Tuairisc came back to me as I watched the boy dance, for he too was from Ballinasloe, Eoghan O Tuairisc having been a shoemaker's son who saw a notice pinned on a tree one day that he'd got first place in a scholarship examination for Garbally Boys' School, then was told he couldn't take up the scholarship for unstated reasons, only being allowed in through the backhand intercession of powerful people in the town, a renowned headmaster at Saint Grellan's National School for instance. He went on to a life of poetry, switching between Gaelic and English, part of the immaculate, the healing heritage of this boy who danced in the arts centre.

Clifden was ragged on a summer night. Harp music coming from a hotel, a ballad being bawled out from a pub opposite the hotel. A few old ladies, scarves on them, walking the streets, picking up bits of gossip from one another. There's no shortage of gossip in Clifden in summer and even in winter sometimes there's excitement – like the winter when an American woman bought the old gaol-house, intending to open it as a hotel for American ghosts. But the plan never worked out and the ghosts stayed on the other side of the Atlantic.

Beyond Clifden, north of it and still in County Galway, is Cleggan. About fifteen years ago I went to a wake in the Pier Bar, the ninety-year-old proprietress laid out, and I said to her sprightly daughter, 'Sorry about the death of your sister.' Tall candles burned about the corpse. Another time in the same pub I saw two small, squat men dance a jig together to celebrate May Day. Seven miles out to sea from Cleggan is Inishbofin. Theodore Roethke lived there for a while, one of the most westerly parts of Galway, but was carted back after a few months, drunk out of his head, in a straitjacket, to the most easterly point of Galway – Ballinasloe Mental Hospital. The conundrum being that Ballinasloe Mental Hospital is actually in Roscommon. Despite this catastrophic vignette there's a serene lyric by Roethke on a plaque in a pub on Bofin:

I suffered for birds, for young rabbits caught in the mower,
My grief was not excessive
For to come upon warblers in early May
Was to forget time and death.

About six o'clock in the morning, my third day in Clifden, the phone rang. My friend's brother-in-law had just died in County Roscommon. There were phone calls made to relatives all over the world. The subject changed. 'The wedding was out of this world.' And by seven one of her sons had arrived in his car and shortly we were racing through the Connemara morning. There are many stories that this county had given me, stories that tumbled out at the worst of times; the story of a ninety-year-old tinker woman who insisted on being brought from Portiuncula Hospital, Ballinasloe, to the side of the road in Aughrim because she said she wanted to die in the open air, and then rose and lived to see Croydon again; my friend the guard in Galway city who on his retirement, only having been out of Ireland once before, working as a labourer on a building site in London in his teens, packed his things in his car, drove to Portugal, and purchased a hut on a beach there where he still lives.

'He brought in a good crop of turf the summer before he left,' the same man had recently commented to me in Portugal about the boy who'd left Ballinasloe when he was sixteen and had since prospered in London – as if his prosperity was a reward for his diligence with the turf. The former guard had been posted in Ballinasloe then. Would that such pleasing omens attended us all. But there is a sense of strength from such language, a trustfulness that mistakes, misfortune can be absolved and that we can start all over again.

'There was a man who lived in a remote part of County Galway and he wasn't very bright and he slept on a hard board. So he got very bad arthritis. The advice he got was to sleep on a feather bed. He put one feather on the floor and slept on it. His arthritis became much worse and he shouted out, "But what would it be like if I slept on a whole bed of feathers!" ' My friend told a story as we raced to the house of the dead man, tinker encampments more profuse in north-east Galway – oilskins thrown over random armchairs – half-wrecked gateposts bearing shaven posters for showbands, pilgrimages to Lourdes, bingo, national schools more isolated and perished-looking, homesteads more beseeching, a congestion of car tyres in one field, and the stories kept coming, long after we'd crossed the border into Roscommon.

North Yemen

It was his first trip back to North Yemen in thirty years. His brother had been killed in a car accident the previous week and had already been buried. The man had lived in the Warrington area of England, working in a cable factory. Qat, the narcotic weed consumed ubiquitously in Yemen – in *mafraj*'s (parlours), behind shop counters, on roadside watches, in modern hotel lounges, the green of a piece of qat forever being revealed in a grin or a scowl – was exported to the north-west of England where many Yemenis live, to fulfil an expatriate Yemeni addiction. The plane descended on a landscape of clefts, hillocks, billowy mountains, an outcast, lunar landscape. The man's tough, leaping curls were stubbed in ash. He wore a black suit, white open-necked shirt. He might not return to England, he said, abandoning his English wife and two children, remaining with his mother.

A day later I passed a funeral outside Sana'a, a body urgently carried on a bier, covered by a jade-green Coswat Al-Kaaba, a party of mirthful children scurrying after the body. Warda, the Egyptian girl singer, keened on the car radio. Most girl singers to be heard in North Yemen are Egyptian. The pin-ups in the windows of drink kiosks beside Bab Al Yaman, the gate to the old city, are of Egyptian girls. Men sit at the tables around the kiosks, drinking lemonade from chipped glasses. Some people claim they saw two men publicly executed by Bab Al Yaman early this year. Others claim that public executions stopped years ago. Some people say they saw two women being lashed for adultery in Taharir Square in January. Others laugh and say this is impossible. Some people inform you in a semi-whisper that a

71

group of blue-movie makers are lying in a dungeon in Sana'a. Others affirm that the blue-movie-making group were never busier, albeit in secret.

In this city of counter-claims, of overlapping realities, one thing that is certain is the power of the *jambia*, the dagger symbol of Yemeni manhood, colourfully swathed over the crotch. The only time I saw people being relieved of it was outside a cinema near Bab Al Yaman where young men were queuing to see *Bruce Lee in New Guinea*, first purchasing a ticket through a tiny porthole from a girl in a yashmak and then raising their arms while a soldier with a scarlet beret on his head scanned their bodies for this piece of Yemeni culture which might not have been so obvious as it usually was. In the square near the queue a goat ate a plastic bag.

'Allah says that drink and girls are bad,' a young man in Pizzeria Carthage on Ali Abdolmoghni Street told me one night. On the street outside there were no girls. A three-legged dog passed. Lights were being ravelled through the trees to prepare for the celebration of Independence Day on 26 September. Some of the lights were already on in this street where the fingers of a few walking pairs of men twitched in a modest grasp. The only public signs of the erotic on this, the main city boulevard, at this time of night are poster collages of famous muscle men, Kevin Von Erich, Tony Atlas, Mil Mascaras. The word *habiba* (sweetheart) was shocking in this atmosphere coming from a gap-toothed Somali boy with a turban on his head. 'Girl or boy?' He crossed the fourth finger of each hand. Then he ran away. There are Somali, Ethiopian, Egyptian prostitutes in this city. In early evening Somali girls walk the streets, often in orange or peach dresses, their heads uncovered, luxuriating in, basking in the sensuality of their bodies and in the foreign notion of female physicality. There is a Rastafarian Ethiopian girl who will get you a prostitute I was told. But late at night the only possible human contact was three boys gaping at a piece of cardboard burning under a tree lit up for the revolution celebrations.

To one side-incline of the city of Old Marib, in the desert east of Sana'a, is a tank abandoned since the civil war (1962–8) when the thousand-year-old Zaidi Imamate, which in its last fifty years blocked North Yemen off from foreigners, was overthrown. The city, city of the Queen of Sheba, spectacularly rises on an elevation above a pale desert, city of mud skyscrapers, ruins locked into one another. Legend is that it began its decline after a deluge engulfed it in the fifth century AD. Now Bedouins live among the ruins. At evening the air is sporadically bitter with the smell of boiling camel's milk. Young men play *caahesh* in the squares of the Sabean city, a game in which wooden sticks are used on a wooden ball. Firelight in the streets, in the houses. Outside the city the evening I visited it three small boys in garments which threatened to consume them sold oranges and biscuits in a crib, an electric light bulb hanging from the ceiling, cards you get in cheese packets in North Yemen around the sides of the crib, cards depicting the Tasmania devil, the Black Buck, the squirrel monkey. Near by is the temple of the Moon Goddess, eight pillars in the sand, remainder of a religion which worshipped sun, moon and evening star. The Three Wise Men would have passed this city, on the Gold and Frankincense Route, following another star. A party of male tourists had come that day from Sana'a to view the temple, crowded into the back of an open truck. Taalb, a little Bedouin boy, had climbed the pillars to impress them. Later I met him among the ruins of Marib, with its occasional awesome Sabean inscriptions, where he lived.

Back in Sana'a that night I sat in the Golden Peacock Restaurant of the Taj Sheba hotel listening to Lebanese songs sung by two Egyptian girls, two Lebanese girls, with hair extravagantly gathered above their heads, in elaborate poodle dresses, dancing. 'Pharmacist, O Pharmacist, give me a medicine for her heart and mine.' A few boys from the Arab Emirates Republic, in sequined jeans, danced on a separate part of the floor, one of them waving a *shal*, the Arab male headdress. The evening ended with a Lebanese song, 'Let's get married.' No one danced to that. The two men at a table near by belonged to National Security.

National Security men stop girls at gunpoint whom they

consider improperly dressed. They follow young men taking
Indian girls for a drive because the Indian girls might be Yemeni
girls. They ask young couples taking a stroll for a marriage
certificate. Foreigners living in the city think they are being
followed through the market of the old city, among the red of
piled-up tamarind, the black of piled-up cloves, between the
yellow and brown nine-storey houses with limewash around the
windows and joyous patterns of white on them, through the
parks littered with debris, past mosque windows through which
you can see huge gatherings of men bow over and over again,
right down to the underground *hamams* – Turkish baths – where
little boys scrupulously scrape the bodies of old men with black,
coarse mittens. National Security men are a joke, a conversation
point, an excuse for an argument in the head.

In Kawkaban, a village outside Sana'a on a mountaintop, I met
a foreigner who was not paranoid and who seemed totally at
home with this society. An Egyptian primary school teacher in a
dun *thoab*, the long Arab shirt. Was he lonely here, I asked. No. A
child walked by on stilts made from cans, strings coming out of
the cans into his hands. In the local hotel a tiny girl in a black
yashmak served Pepsi Cola. Cairo, city of gurkies, of sagpipes, of
riverside wedding groups, was a long way away. The village
water tank had an inscription on it from the Qur'an. 'Everything
was created from water.' But I felt this place was arid and wanted
to get away from it.

In my time in Sana'a more and more lights went up, pending
the revolution celebrations. During the days I visited far-flung
regions, towns, villages. In Djibla, home of the most unbiddable
of Muslem queens, Queen Arwa, I sat in a boy's bedroom,
leaning on a *makrat* – a cushion – playing *kiram*, the black and
white television showing a Kuwaiti soap opera, as the wedding
of the boy's sister was being celebrated upstairs. I couldn't go
and look because it was just women who were celebrating today.
A girl went up and reported back. The bride sat silently in a room
with her mother, blue, black, pink make-up on her, a gold band
through her hair with nasturtiums hanging out of it, a blue veil
running around the back of her head. In a room further up,

women, their faces exposed, inhaled from a hubble-bubble, sipped blackberry juice. The following day the men would celebrate in the man's house, chewing qat. The bride would repair to the man's house that evening but wouldn't meet him and go to bed with him until the evening after that, again because qat chewing, once begun, takes a long time. Immediately after the first night the bride and groom, accompanied by a party of men, would journey to a stream in this countryside of illuminated sugar-cane terraces while the women made cakes at home for the ultimate celebration where women and men joined up. At no stage would there have been an actual wedding ceremony. The joining together was a kind of innuendo from these celebrations.

North of Sana'a are the Haraz mountains, very much like the Himalayas, and Indian Muslim settlers, the Bhoras, have made their home here, building mosques on mountaintops. Sunlight creeps over the red carpets in mosques. Young men race along mountain ledges on motorbikes. The countryside swims here. It is peaceful, hopeful. Old men kneel on hilltops and say they are praying to Allah in the skies. In one of the highest mountaintop villages, Al-Hajara, a little boy took me by the hand and dashed with me to the elevated centre of the village, had me climb to the top of a nine-storey house to meet his mother. She was bent over the *haar* – Yemeni stove – making bread. She was without her yashmak. Her face was ravaged, bony, but her eyes, like his, were a startling blue. She quickly seized her yashmak, put it on, took it off again, put it on again, then eventually took it off for the last time during my visit and stood on the balcony, against the green herbs lining the balcony wall, her lemon head veil and her blue dress blowing dramatically.

In Street Number Nine off Taharir Square in Sana'a there was a woman, who ran a small grocery store, who always wore the smallest of yashmaks but who still always managed to have an elaborately patterned crimson or gold dress on, in contrast to the generally uniform black which muffles women in this city. People said she'd been wild in her youth but now had reformed and had four children. Only one evening she wasn't merry and flashing radiance in her eyes, slumped over her counter. 'I was drunk,' she laughed the next night. Most women in North Yemen wear the yashmak, *lathmah, hejab* as it is variously called. Women from the Tihama district near the sea don't and these, dark-skinned women in dusty black with shining lines of gold in it, were the only ones I saw begging, in a village outside Sana'a, making a joke of it, exchanging sly grins to one another during their exhortations for money. Some boys began throwing stones at them and they vigorously threw stones back.

On Street Number Nine I would eat fenugreek and egg at a table outside the café of Mr Mohammed Al-Reemi. Then I'd repair to the café of Mr Mhub Coffe where I'd have a drink of hot milk and a slice of flat sponge cake, the milk boiled in a huge well-worn saucepan over a gas flame. At eleven o'clock each night a troupe of young men would come in for hot milk and sponge cake, sitting decorously and quietly around a table. In a country which bans alcohol their order is equivalent to the last round.

All the lights were up for the revolution celebrations at the end of my visit, tangled through trees, threaded on the front of buildings. The Yemeni colours, oblong black, white, scarlet with a black star in the middle, were sported on the front of motor bikes. The moustached face of the President, Mr Abdullah As Sallal, was on every second car, in every second shop window. The woman in the grocery store on Street Number Nine was wearing a vermilion dress. Otherwise women had long disappeared from view in Sana'a. In this night of coloured lights, of social expectancy, she looked at me keenly and reproached me.

'*Thaa baad al sokar vi ainac.*'

'Put some sugar in your eyes.'

1989

In Russia

'It's not like they say it is. Guns and bombs. It's just people talking like this.' It was two in the morning in a hotel in Novgorod, a town where Hitler had not left one residential house standing and, in the Middle Ages, where Theophanes the Greek, having left the companionship of the ikon maker Andrei Rublev in Moscow, had come to fill the walls of the many churches with frescos.

The young man, athletic-looking and contained as a circus acrobat, was wearing a sleeveless white vest. On his wrist a tattoo indicating the initials of Soviet Troops serving in Germany. His family, those who did not live in Italy and France, had been eliminated in the Armenian earthquake. He was a refugee here. Apart from having served in Germany, he'd been on the front in Afghanistan and that's what he was referring to now.

'The talking like this' was people around us pouring Scotch whisky, Armenian cognac, Armenian brandy, down their mouths. At four in the morning he banged on my door, roubles in his outstretched hands. Did I have any drink? It was all gone, I pleaded. Anyway just then some rather hesitant-looking Soviet girls appeared at the top of the stairs to comfort him.

Next day in Café Posad in Novgorod, a basement, rouge-lit café, I listened to protest songs against the war in Afghanistan. A man and his wife hear their son is joining the army. Then they hear he's being sent to Afghanistan. Then they hear he's been killed. *Men Who Dance the Disco*, an Indian film, and *Men From Outer Space*, a Japanese film, were showing at the October Cinema. Outside it young people told me how they planned to fake medical certificates to avoid the war. Young people here guilefully protest and the authorities don't seem to mind.

In Leningrad they smoke Ukrainian and Afghan hash in the streets, in little cars pulled up outside the teeming market on Kuznechnyy Lane, a market where the healing karina and boyjaryshnik berries are on sale in great mounds. One of these cars revved off while I was in it and ultimately, after a stop for a meal, brought me to a flat in the outskirts of Leningrad. The flat belonged to a professor but one of the group illegally rented a room in it. The bath was beside the kitchen sink. Ereni the Airedale ran riot.

The boy sub-let his room in the evenings to couples who wished to make love. We encountered one such couple. The girl was thrown out into the snow but the boy joined us to listen to Sting, 'Moon Over Bourbon Street', 'Consider Me Gone', under the Stars and Stripes of the '76 Gasoline Company and to drink champagne we'd bought in the Metropole Restaurant where Rasputin had once dined, where waiters offer to sell you caviare from under their jackets or to change money, where women in fur hats rock and roll to 'Rock Around the Clock' or tango to Cole Porter's 'I'll String Along With You'.

A buxom bag of hashish was taken out. A student at the Electro-Technical Institute talked about his pen-pal girlfriend whom he'd encountered on Nevsky Prospect when he'd tried to sell her caviare – Natasha, Russian descendant from Merthyr Tydfil.

Early next morning in a café, christened the Gastric Café because of the bad food, a girl told me a folk story, illustrating it all the time on napkins. 'When becomes a spring there was born a farmer's son.' We said goodbye outside Café Saigon. I was going back to Moscow for Christmas Day, which in Russia is on 7 January.

Yelokhovsky Cathedral was crowded on Christmas Eve. Red carnations were everywhere pushed among bits of Christmas tree. Old women dipped to kiss an ikon showing the Adoration of the Magi. A pool of old women sang hymns before the same ikon, crossing themselves again and again and bowing their heads again and again. Two women haggled over candles, one pulling them off the stand when they were only half-depleted, the other grabbing them and putting them on again.

During the service itself the Patriarch of Moscow with his flowing snow beard stood directly in front of the crowd and blessed it. I was reminded of the blessing at Levin's wedding in *Anna Karenina*: 'They prayed that God would make them fruitful and bless them as he blessed Isaac and Rebecca, Joseph, Moses and Zipporah and that they might look upon their children's children.'

I'd seen Tolstoy's bicycle in a house near an outdoor heated swimming pool where you can swim with the snow falling on top of you, where men exercise on the ice at the sides, and where old women with fake pink roses in their bathing caps jump up and down in the water, beseeching the snow with outstretched, generally puny arms.

At the toll of New Year on Red Square a troupe of elderly male and female joggers had appeared from nowhere, some in fancy dress, and had jogged across the square, disappearing behind St Basil's Cathedral. They do this every New Year, jogging from one end of Moscow to the other, magically appearing on Red Square at the stroke of midnight.

I'd said goodbye to the old year in my own way. The day before the Red Square celebrations I'd taken a train from Kiev Railway Station to visit the grave of Boris Pasternak. In Peredelkino, first watching children take rides on amusement swans and horses in an alcove of the station, watching boys elsewhere play games of Moscow boys – machines where you sink submarines with sudden illuminations of torpedoes.

Pasternak had stayed in Russia but at the grave in the expiring light of a year which in some ways had been the worst in my life, Christmas decorations on many of the graves, I was reminded of the words of someone who'd left Russia, Marc Chagall. 'To preserve the earth in one's roots or to rediscover other earth, that is a true miracle.'

There were many visual miracles in this country; young soldiers chewing tinsel like hay as they talk to you, a little boy

holding a lighted candle over a book of hymns before the Magi
Ikon in Yelokhovsky Cathedral, the successive flames of candles
in glass cases containing bunches of red carnations along the
snow-piled streets outside Kiev Railway Station.

And by Pasternak's grave I was able to ponder for the first time
an anecdote told to me by a vicar from Richmond just before our
plane had landed in Russia, an anecdote which seemed to be at
home here.

A few days before Christmas in England, late at night, a young
man had knocked on the vicar's door. He was a lance-corporal
from Northern Ireland who'd deserted the day he discovered he
had Aids. He'd been sleeping in Richmond Park, afraid to go to
Dorset to reveal his double shame to his parents.

British Airways had played 'There's no Place Like Home at
Christmas' as the plane had touched down into the snow and
forest-tapestries of Russia. On the other side of the airport barrier
an old woman had waited with a bunch of red carnations.

Lisbon

There is something ceremonial about the way the managers of
the most established cafés in Lisbon arrange the gladioli on
Saturday mornings in early summer, for instance at A Brasileira
high up above Rossio, Lisbon's main square, at Pastelaria Suica
on Rossio where the waitress will offer you a volume of different
ice-cream illustrations, and at the oldest café of all, Nicola's, also
on Rossio, which dates from the eighteenth century. Manuel
Maria Barbosa Du Bocage, Portugal's wild-cat poet of the late
eighteenth century, used to have his coffee there and he is
depicted in a variety of murals on the walls, taking his beloved
for a stroll, haranguing the clergy. Inside, waiters in formal black
and white serve coffee. The atmosphere is Berlin 1930s. What's
gone from the rest of Europe – Prague is an exception – survives
in these pockets of Lisbon, elegant cafés, languorous, sprucely
dressed coffee drinkers, eyes that agilely take in everybody
around. If you're new to Lisbon it's better to sit outside where
you'll be served Nicola's special white wine by a waiter in white
and where you can watch the street hawkers. Later, while you
wander in the square, if you look the part you'll be offered a
choice of hash or whisky.

Like Porto to the north, Lisbon is a city of red roofs. It rises in
an entranced way above the Tagus. Red roofs; leaden, terracotta,
khaki fronts; dashes of verdure at the sides of houses, in street
corners; gable windows open with a theatrical display of newly
blanched ladies' underwear. It is a city a very grumpy Henry
Fielding confronted in a different guise, when he came here
searching for a cure from various ailments before the earthquake
of 1755. He died complaining about the city and as the British

weren't interested in marking his grave the French consul seized the initiative and placed a tomb in 1786 – for the honour of Fielding and the honour of France! A gentle and helpful English vicar will show you the tomb if you knock politely on the door of the presbytery alongside the English cemetery – a giant edifice, sun snatching the outlines of cypress trees behind it.

Lisbon is full of street sights. The man who gets his cat to play with – and even caress – a hamster and a pigeon on the pavements. The little blind woman with the tossed, 1960s hairstyle who sings Fado songs, beating all the time on her triangle. She moves between Rossio and Rua dos Pescadores in Costa da Caparica, the seaside resort just south of Lisbon.

For lunch, for a change from the old cafés, you should go to the Calouste Gulbenkian Modern Art Centre, next to the extravagant Gulbenkian gardens, where you can have gloriously arrayed macrobiotic food among young people, many of whom will seem to have walked out of the José De Almada Negreiros, the Lino António paintings upstairs – concentrated groups, stylized posturings of the legs, often strung 1920s high heels on a girl's feet.

After lunch you can take a train from Cais do Sodre to Estoril and Cascais, by little stations flooded by bougainvillaea, to these resorts where the sea is flanked by *fin de siècle* buildings, overwatched by the occasional ice-cream-like turret. But despite the loveliness of the trip you'll meet too many tourists at the end of the journey so my advice is, for a more exhilarating afternoon, to take the ferry over the Tagus from Cais do Sodre – passing under Sul Ponte, Salazar's dream – to Cacilhas where you can take a bus to Costa da Caparica, where the people of Lisbon go and where you'll rarely encounter a foreign tourist.

But before you leave Cais do Sodre look at the flower vendors, ladies with poodles in cardboard boxes beside them selling red roses. Don't be put off in Caparica by the high-rise apartment buildings rearing over the sea or by the swarms of Nivea sellers. This is where cabals of Lisbon young people sleep on the cement between surfing bouts and where the skin of Lisbon ladies ventures mango colour. For ultimate exaltation in season you can take a toy train for about eight kilometres down the coast, with a choice of nineteen beaches, the railway-side broken by straw-hut cafés, each one with its own pet palm tree beside it. On beach Number 17 you can play badminton in the nude, flitting over to the straw-hut café for refreshments of wine.

At evening try the house speciality in the Nova Perola, the market café and restaurant in Caparica – boiled *bacalhau* (salted cod), with boiled cauliflower, boiled potatoes, a hard-boiled egg and a clove of garlic. The market people come in for wine, for brandies and the odd dog tries to break the barricade – the six-year-old son of the proprietor whose job it is to shoo him off – and come in to beg. By now Rua dos Pescadores, which connects the beach with the market place, will be alive with night strollers; no evident rush among some of the strollers to shed surfing wear.

One Saturday night in June I watched people dance on the esplanade in Caparica as a man on a platform heartily sang 'I want to make love with dew.' Old ladies who looked as though they were just in from pilgrimages to Fatima danced with their near-infant sons, young women danced with young women, old men with old men; nearby boys doing acrobatics with bikes above the sea tried, with little success, to divert attention.

But you may want to go back to eat in Lisbon. The place to head for is Bairro Alto, above Rossio, where there is a flourishing amount of washing hanging out, often over café doors. The fire of autumn 1988 was associated with Bairro Alto but in fact it only burned down a commercial street – a street of shops and warehouses – leading from Rossio to Bairro Alto. It means that part of the way you will have to walk a ramp from Rossio to Bairro Alto. Old ladies, often in pale blue, with russet hair, a brooch in the shape of a cockle at their breasts, gaze at the ruins and mumble to themselves before they move on for gossip and coffee at A Brasileira with women who look like them. The ruins from the topmost point of the ramp do look staggering, the street below almost entirely gutted here, understandably eliciting exclamations under the breath from meandering, bountifully if haphazardly adorned ladies.

In Bairro Alto, further on and higher up from A Brasileira at

Rua Garrett, there is a fecundity of restaurants and cafés among the crammed, hilly streets. Bars where you often have to peer through the washing to see what's happening inside. Bota Alta, at the top of Travessa da Queimada, is a restaurant where people dine among porcelain boots, boots with patterns of flowers on them, extravagantly high laced boots, a boot with a porcelain mouse sitting in it, his legs outstretched, a boot with the message 'I love Rio' on it. But the queue for tables might be too long – the fabulist décor famed – and if it is you'll have a choice of lots of other less fashionable restaurants, places where the television is often on but where you can eat *bacalhau*, squid or *espadarte* – swordfish – and receive unflustered attention.

Afterwards you can look down from Bairro Alto at a city where in June the jacaranda is a solid fog in the night, where the neon of the Scandinavian, the Nicaraguan, the Rotterdam, the Liverpool, the Texas bars – since preserved from the taint of fire – sidle into one another.

If you're tired and don't feel like the walk up to Bairro Alto there is a little restaurant off Rossio, Cervejaria Mariscos Restaurante, where good food will be thrust at you, where people dawdle endlessly each night, backsides slumberously thrust out, and the odd artistically ravaged drunk comes in to make a fuss, only to be thrown out in a way that half invites him to come in again.

Often in Lisbon as you're waiting for a bus at night, especially further out, there'll be a kiosk near by, lit by a gas lamp, cluttered with bottles, with seething packets of crisps, where you can purchase a brandy to say goodnight to this lovely, sensually ever-alive and – by and large – rock-bottom cheap city.

Eerie distant light:
the writings of Marguerite Yourcenar

My first visit to the United States I hitchhiked from San Francisco to Clairmont near Los Angeles to give a reading. After my reading a man, a lecturer at the college, gave me a poem he said he'd gotten from a Hungarian children's writer he'd once encountered in a forest in Mexico. After that I had an appointment to meet a runaway from Ireland, a girl. The venue was a mauve-painted wooden house high above Point Lobos where Robert Louis Stevenson had sojourned. By coincidence, this was the home of the Hungarian the academic had met in the Mexican forest. The old man, a disciple of Gurdjieff, black beret on his head and a Santa Claus beard which sprouted out over a crisp red checked shirt and under eyes that seemed to stare out from an enmeshment of thoughts, had left Hungary when he was twenty-six. He'd brought with him to America a collection of poems by the Hungarian poet Endre Ady and it was one of these poems he'd translated which had been the gift, the almost ritualistic gift by all accounts, in the Mexican forest.

> I am as everyman, Majesty, North Pole.
> Mystery, Strangeness.
> Eerie distant light.
> Eerie distant light.

And reading Marguerite Yourcenar, another escapee from Europe, who lived for fifty years by the ocean on the other side of America, I continually recalled those lines which had been infused for me by the experience of Point Lobos – lighthouses, the Pacific with its baskets of surf rhythmically rolling in and, if you get close, seals always rising in the water. Yes, her intimate, her almost conniving sympathy with animals was part of it. 'A hare which my young hunter had tamed with great effort was caught and torn by the hounds, sole woe of shadowless days.' In another book a hare is sent back to his late medieval roaming ground where the air is mellifluously cadenced by 'the wood-pecker's drill and the jay's cry' rather than be cooked for dinner; lions who mangle criminals in ancient Rome incommodiously weep for the dog who lived with them and has been taken away from them. A young white Russian girl spits in the face of the sexually withheld young man she is in love with under a critical object – a motheaten squirrel in a vest and Tyrolese hat.

Marguerite Yourcenar elevates the vulnerability of all living things and vouches over and over again, painfully, with auster-ity, for the majesty of everyman, be he philosopher or labourer, against a world which has violence on all sides of it, a world, for all its occasional lushness, she finally admitted she felt was 'without a future'.

As with John Berger, history for Marguerite Yourcenar is always contemporary, always in parallel with our own lives, but for her it has a more mystical sense to it. For her all history lives deep within us so that by those secret areas touched, those areas activated by a brew of will-power and divine intervention, we can journey back randomly, can treat ourselves to diorama-views of other ages. By invoking scenes of history she endeavours to decipher our present age 'without a future' and perhaps by so doing, by the chiaroscuro graft upon graft of historical parallel, she gives it a chance of rescue.

In *The Abyss* (1968) religious frenzy and zeal are shown disintegrating into madness, the Anabaptists who have taken over the city of Munster having elected a leader who is ghoulish, *mardi-gras* and greedy in a way we would recognize all too readily now. There's a familar showmanship in his greed.

The first official mourning was for the death of Jan Matthyjs, killed while leading thirty men (and a host of angels) in a sortie attempted against the Bishop's army. Immediately after this disaster, Hans Bockhold was proclaimed Prophet King; wearing a royal crown and mounted on a horse irreverently caparisoned with a chasuble, he took office on the open space before the church. Soon a platform was erected where the new David sat enthroned each morning, rendering decisions without appeal on matters both terrestrial and celestial. A few felicitous excursions, which had overturned the Bishop's kitchen tents and produced a booty of pigs and hens, were occasion for a feast on this platform, accompanied by the music of fifes; when the enemy's kitchen boys, taken prisoner, were forced to prepare the viands and then were killed by the pommeling and kicking of the crowd, Hilzonda laughed with the rest of the company.

In *Memoirs of Hadrian* (1951) the Emperor Hadrian watches Antinous, his boy lover, being buried, the pompous incarceration underground. The seeming passivity of death is meditated upon and wrested with, by the force and even the mania of the meditation thus challenged, a challenge which reverberates, which ricochets with almost one voice, with one quest, through the whole of Marguerite Yourcenar's fiction.

The youth from Claudiopolis was descending into the tomb like a Pharaoh, or a Ptolemy. There we left him, alone. He was entering upon that endless tenure, without air, without light, without change of season, compared with which every life seems short; such was the stability to which he had attained, such perhaps was the peace. Centuries as yet unborn within the dark womb of time would pass by thousands over that tomb without restoring life to him, but likewise without adding to his death, and without changing the fact he had been.

Hadrian, like Marguerite Yourcenar, is a mixture of races, Spanish by birth, Roman by parentage, Greek by inclination. He scours the known world, fretting from landscape to landscape, from one hue to another, always approximating, knowing one apparently decisive landscape is inveigled by three or four other landscapes, that national blood is always linked with that of three or four other nationalities.

Born Belgian, of a French father, Marguerite Yourcenar adventurously travelled Europe between the wars, probably in 'a third class seat in those carriages reserved since time immemorial for prophets, for the poor, for soldiers on leave, for messiahs'. Just before the war she left for the United States where she settled on an island off Maine, finding special empathy in her new country with the Blacks of the Southern States, an eloquent, keening people. Likewise Zeno, the Reformation scientist hero of *The Abyss*, determinedly travels Europe from north to south, dipping into the Orient which provides him with an all-important whiff of Sufi philosophy, coming as it does from the Dervish Derazi, a dissident like Zeno, in his case a Muslim dissident, a refraction in the way Marguerite Yourcenar peoples the world with refractions, sometimes even, at heightened moments of flight, the one person breaking down into a kaleidoscope of refractions, the journey invoking multiples of people within the one journey-crazed person, giving an epic dimension, beloved of the kind of historian Marguerite Yourcenar is, to the one frail being.

An object brought from Italy was hanging on the wall of the small antechamber, a Florentine mirror in a tortoise-shell frame, formed from a combination of some twenty little convex mirrors hexagonal in shape, like the cells of a beehive, and each mirror enclosed, in its turn, by a narrow border which had once been the shell of a living creature. Zeno looked at himself there in the grey light of a Parisian dawn. What he saw was twenty figures compressed and reduced by the laws of optics, twenty images of a man in a fur bonnet, of haggard and sallow complexion, with gleaming eyes which were themselves mirrors. The man in flight, enclosed within a world of his own, separated from others like himself who were also in flight in worlds parallel to his, recalled to him the hypothesis of the Greek Democritus, about an infinite series of identical universes in each of which lives and dies imprisoned a series of philosophers.

At one point in Zeno's journeys, as if in retort to Hadrian's meditations on death, he accompanies an old monk who searches through the charcoaled remains of a Jew burned to death, for the 'luz', the bone which cannot be consumed, the axiom of the resurrection, the seed which makes the individual what is for the moment 'the inaccesible fire of the stars'.

The stars play a dynamic part in the fiction of Marguerite Yourcenar. One can imagine that when she made her home on Mount Desert Island, terrain which reeked of mysterious Indian civilizations, the Micmac and Abenaki who would once appear there during the fishing season, she must have had spectacular views of the stars, views which one would never have got in Europe and which would have inspired passages in *Memoirs of Hadrian* and *The Abyss* – the stars as pulverizers of time, outlying vistas of them cohering the perspective of the centuries, making the moment to hand diamond, riveting in its possibilities.

> Here at the Villa I have built an observatory, but I can no longer climb its steps. Once in my life I did a rarer thing. I made a sacrifice to the constellations of an entire night. It was after my visit to Osroes, coming back through the Syrian desert: lying on my back, wide awake but abandoning for some hours every human concern, I gave myself up from nightfall to dawn to this world of crystal and flame. That was the most glorious of all my voyages. (*Memoirs of Hadrian.*)

At other times the stars are magical but misleading in their allure – those who are unduly fascinated by them are those who don't know their own heart and will betray you.

> All that winter, high up between the lake's frozen plains and the cold sky, peering from the recess of a tall window, the philosopher would compute the positions of such stars as might bring good or bad fortune to the house of Vasa. He was aided in this task by the heir to the throne, young Prince Eric, for whom these dangerous sciences held an unwholesome attraction. In vain did Zeno remind him that the stars, though they influence our destinies, do not determine them: and that

our lives are regulated by the heart, that fiery star palpitating in the dark of our bodies, suspended there in its cage of flesh and bone, as strong and mysterious as the stars above, and obeying laws more complicated than the laws we make ourselves. (*The Abyss*)

Sex – settling in beside someone ('with the tranquillity of a spouse'), 'the sound of a cry' in love-making, the 'ardent love of the human body' – can be a foothold to an experience of the eternal, can annihilate for moments our apparent imprisonment in time. But of all areas in Marguerite Yourcenar's fiction the area of sex is the most changeable, the meditation on it the most quixotic. For Hadrian sensuality is religion.

I have sometimes thought of constructing a system of human knowledge which would be based on eroticism, a theory of contact wherein the mysterious value of each being is to offer to us just that point of perspective which another world affords. In such a philosophy pleasure would be a more complete but also specialized form of approach to the other, one more technique of getting to know what is not ourselves. In the least sensual encounters it is still in our contacts that emotion begins, or ends; the somewhat repugnant hand of the old woman who presents me her petition, the moist brow of my father in death's agony, the wound I wash for an injured soldier.

But for the next of Marguerite Yourcenar's great heroes, Zeno, sex, like Eric the son of the King of Sweden, is a betrayer.

For he continued to consider love's burning mysteries as the only means of access for many of us to that fiery realm of which we are perhaps the infinitesimal sparks. But the sublime ascent of such experience is of brief duration, and he wondered whether an act so subject to material routines, and so dependent upon the instruments of physical generation, is not a thing for the philosopher to try, but then to renounce thereafter. Chastity, which he had once viewed as a superstition to be fought, now appeared to him as one aspect of his serenity:

that detached understanding which one has of others when one no longer desires them was greatly to his liking.

When Zeno finds tranquillity, in anonymity, in Bruges, helping the poor through his profession as a doctor it is the world of eroticism which betrays his tranquillity, a world his young monk-helper becomes absorbed in – the interpretation is Gnostic, the experience is rapturous, the methods are fascinating but they lead to death, to downfall, the shattering of a prolonged serenity.

> . . . a fair damsel enters a fountain's basin to bathe, accompanied by her lovers; two other lovers, revealed only by the position of their bare feet, are embracing behind a curtain. A youth tenderly parts the knees of a beloved object who resembles him like a brother. From the mouth and private orifice of a boy, prostrate on hands and knees, branch delicate flowers, growing up towards the heavens. A Moorish maiden carries a gigantic red raspberry on a tray.

The young musician in *Alexis* (1929) sees the denial of sex as sin; during his genteel upbringing in Austria he thought a less lonely existence would be more pure. But for a similiar hero of an early novel, the young Prussian officer afloat among White Russians in *Coup de Grâce* (1939), his own strangeness is less a love of boys than a love of solitude. Throughout these early novels, whether in sex or in solitude, one is aware in these characters of what Frederick Prokosch calls 'deep, unshatterable innocence'. Later it is more complicated, the attitude to sex is shirty. 'Names (like sodomite) bear no relation to facts; they stand only for what the herd imagines.' (*The Abyss*) And at possibly the overall moment of crescendo in the fiction of Marguerite Yourcenar, the death of the simple, labouring, seventeenth-century man Nathaniel in *An Obscure Man* (1982), there is what seems like testimony, concessions to sexuality but acknowledgement of androgyny as wisdom.

He had, rarely it is true, known the carnal brootherhood other men had shared with him; he didn't feel less a man for that.

People falsify everything, it seemed to him, in taking such little account of the flexibility and resources of the human being, so like the plant which seeks out the sun or water and nourishes itself fairly well from whatever earth the wind has sown in it. Custom more than nature seemed to him to dictate the differences set up between classes of men, the habits and knowledge acquired from infancy, or the ways of praying to what is called God. Ages, sex, or even species seemed to him closer one to another than each generally assumed about the other: child or old man, man or woman, animal or biped who speaks and works with his hands, all came together in the misery and sweetness of existence.

Just as Marguerite Yourcenar says of Cavafy's Antony, that he was in love with Alexandria more than with Cleopatra, so it very often seems that Hadrian is more in love with the landscapes in which his affair is happening rather than with the person himself. And it is to a landscape much like Mount Desert Island, in a *Das Lied von der Erde* accumulation of atmosphere, that the penultimate of Marguerite Yourcenar's heroes comes to die, a death as total in its description as the death of J.T. Malone in Carson McCullers's *Clock Without Hands*, which is prefigured by an ever greater emphasis on the physical, the 'egg in the milkshake' for instance. 'The death of each man is like him,' Chekhov says. What Nathaniel's death tells us, maybe, is that it's best to live simply, to make simple, everyday things our mainstay, that art, as Bruce Chatwin finally reminded us, 'always lets you down'.

'Dear God, when shall I die?' Right from the outset of Marguerite Yourcenar's fiction there's this obsession with death, with lying down. In the tumult of Nathaniel's approaching death words, vocabulary, books, the idea of them, are discarded.

But it seemed to him now that the books he had managed to read (should one judge all books by them?) had given him very little, less perhaps than the enthusiasm or thought he had brought to them; in any case, he considered it would be wrong not to concentrate on the world he had in front of him, now

94

and for so little time to come, and which had, as it were, fallen to him by chance. To read books was like swigging brandy: it was a way of numbing oneself into not being there.

Sometimes reservations are set aside and words are the most rapturous of human creative possibilities.

Magic, above all, is the virulent force of words, which are always stronger than the things for which they stand: their power justifies what is said about them in Sepher Yetsira, not to mention between us the Gospel According to Saint John.

But even early on, in *Alexis*, words are found brutally inadequate to describe cataclysm. 'Words serve so many people, Monique, that they are no longer useful to anyone.' Even Zeno, sage, philospher, alchemist, doctor, tells us that he has 'almost come to the point of distrusting words'. In one of his bids to escape his terrible destiny, to shake it off, he begins a journey on a country lane and in the strange calm that sometimes sets in at moments when circumstances seem to ask for disturbance he finds that words, concepts lift from him and that he is at peace.

For a moment he called to mind the alchemical concept of viriditas, of the innocent piercing through of Being from within the nature of things, a blade of life in its purest form; but then he ceased to pursue all such thoughts in order to give himself over entirely to the purity of the morning.

Paul Klee wrote of his art in similar terms.

In a forest, I have felt many times over that it was not I who looked at the forest. Some days I felt that the trees were looking at me, were speaking to me . . . I was listening . . . I think that the painter must be penetrated by the universe and not want to penetrate it . . . I expect to be inwardly submerged, buried. Perhaps I paint to break out.

The creation of the character of Zeno, the most weighty of Marguerite Yourcenar's characterizations, was partly inspired by Leonardo da Vinci, and D. H. Lawrence's partial opprobium for

Leonardo comes to mind when I am confronted with some of Zeno's self-wrangles.

There is, I think, this strain of cold dislike, or self-dislike, through much of the Renaissance art, and through all the later Shakespeare. In Shakespeare it is a kind of corruption in the flesh and a conscious revolt from this. A sense of corruption in the flesh makes Hamlet frenzied for he will never admit that it is his own flesh. Leonardo da Vinci is the same, but Leonardo loves the corruption maliciously. Michelangelo rejects any corruption, he stands by the flesh, the flesh only.[1]

Zeno is both a Leonardo and a Michelangelo; he savours both these opposite reactions and perhaps this is some of the clue to the English title *The Abyss*, the abyss between sensual totality and intellectual hesitance, as it is between thought and word, the route of identity Sophie in *Coup de Grâce* takes between White Russia and the Bolsheviks, between counterfeit, short-changed self and real, heroic self, for real self is always heroic for Marguerite Yourcenar as it was for Pasternak.

Never mind. That disjunction, that break in continuity, that 'night of the soul' which so many of us experienced at the time, each in his own way (and so often in far more tragic and final form than I did), was essential, perhaps in order to force me into trying to bridge not only the distance which separated me from Hadrian, but, above all, the distance which separated me from my true self.

Marguerite Yourcenar's fiction, taken as a visionary whole, scrupulously signposts the route through self-deceit, sabotaged potential, to luminous, to heroic, to majestic, although very often doomed, self.

Contemplating Etruscan effigies in Italy Lawrence, who elsewhere splenetically felt that we have many souls, was struck by this life force which exists from birth to death. 'So within each man is the quick of him, when he is a baby, and when he is old,

[1] *Twilight in Italy*

the same quick: some spark, some unborn and undying vivid life-electron.'[1] From her own struggle against assaults on this life-electron Marguerite Yourcenar gives us talismans not just to protect it in ourselves but to reacquaint ourselves with it: the furrow of a river in a medieval landscape, the whiff of cherry brandy in the air, the resonance of eglantine placed between the pages of a book.

Hadrian saw our world as one always bound to self-destroy and be born again from chaos; art is the major regenerator and, with the epic view of her art as well as its personal one, Marguerite Yourcenar is a builder in Yeats's sense, an almost naïve connotation of the word now.

> All things fall and are built again
> And those that build them again are gay.

My first visit to the United States, shortly after an experience of Belfast and street killings there, I walked among beach nasturtiums on the Californian coast. The nasturtiums trembled with light. For moments I had escaped; the fire of the nasturtiums, the palpitations in them on a clear day, was a transcendence. Those seaboard nasturtiums, a snowy-bearded Hungarian with plaintive, almost tremulous cat's eyes under a black beret, make me think now of Marguerite Yourcenar, someone who understood violence and not only went beyond it but created a force of beauty in that domain beyond it which might help to barter, in Dostoevsky's sense of redemptive beauty, a world which is mostly horrible but still offers perspectives of the Pacific, the surf rolling in, dark verdure immortalized by Robert Louis Stevenson sloping down to it, and the odd seal lifting his head, in a kind of sympathy with us, above the surf.

Like Lawrence, like Faulkner, like Christ, 'the man with hair infected by a vermin of stars', whose teachings are 'not unlike those of Orpheus', by the intensity of her words she creates a beauty to combat the attacks of chaos and makes us understand the unity of all historical epochs, the 'lilies of the field', the 'wild

[1] *Etruscan Places*

flower' of every epoch; she penetrates the mysterious veil between time and eternity as Hadrian did for moments in Syria on a night of 'crystal and flame', as two boy lovers do, lying arms outstretched to create wings in the snow; she guides us to the precipice of a world an old Brahmin joined with when he threw himself into a fire, leaving the melancholy echo of a woman's song in the desert night.

Prague

'The Czechoslovak people don't understand Petersburg, they don't understand Kiev, they don't understand Rostov-on-Don,' Victoria, a romantic-minded Russian lady with hair in a pigtail, told me one evening in U Modré Štiky on Karlova Street in Prague. She was from Rostov-on-Don. She'd come to Prague as wife of a Czech man whom she subsequently divorced but she was going to stay in Prague until her two boys were educated and then return to Russia. A young man at our table, for some reason, kept drawing images from the suburbs of Prague – high-rise flats, factories – on napkins, packing a napkin with images before discarding it for another. A middle-aged man at another table got up to go but fell flat on his face, drunk. Afterwards, on the street, a stranger picked a bone of something called Minsky trout from my forehead, the bone having become entangled there during the conversation. The night before I left Prague I heard my name called on the street. It was Victoria. She was with her small, chubby son Alexander. He was in a T-shirt with the word 'Scene' on it. Victoria kept touching her nose with a bunch of basil. Both of them reached hands to me to wish me farewell and hope I'd be back soon to this city which obviously troubled Victoria but whose possibilities of adventure in the form of restaurant encounters fixated her.

The picture of the Crimean coast at the entrance to the washrooms at Prague airport prepares you. The most mundane area is edified by beauty. A notice board – rooms advertised – has pictures of a boy hugging a boxer dog, a robin over a clump of pansies as decorations. There is a fake cello in the window of a dry cleaner's. A boy has his arm in a sling but the sling is striking red with patterns of cobalt in it. From Prague airport, if you arrive independently, you take the 119 bus to Leninova and there take the metro to the centre where, if you're searching for accommodation, you go to Pragotur, beside the Gothic, charred-looking Powder Tower. There was a broom at the back of the red bus the day I took it. I'd last been here in August two years before. Pragotur will fix you up with a Czech family or you might be lucky and get a shabby room with a picture of a pharaoh in it in the Meteor Hotel, up the road from Pragotur on Hybernska Street, a hotel which sells champagne and toothbrushes alongside one another in the foyer. It's best to present yourself early in the morning. This time I spent a few days at the Meteor and a few days with a Czech doctor and her husband in the hills of Suchdol outside Prague, men drinking beer outside hut-like *vinarnas* on the way. Revealing though that stay was, I found it better to be in the Meteor, in easy reach of the places of conversation late at night.

Resplendent, silvery-grey boulevards converge on a sudden clutter of yellow-ochre or primrose houses, red roofs on them, the odd onion dome splattered in the architectural mêlée, a baroque gable craning to be seen. Tableaux appear on these most unlikely edges of these houses – the Annunciation above a pub door, an apparition of the Virgin among cornfields not far from an ice-cream window, a Tarot-like queen dominating the amber of a square at evening. From hilltops on the castle side of Prague in May you could look down at troughs of red or peach roofs and immaculate acacia blossom. At evening sometimes, along the river, the beauty is almost heart-breaking, silhouetted outline of towers and domes on the other side, a vermilion gesticulation of sunset clouds behind the castle, a few dozen swans beating their way along just above the water.

Irony, an almost malicious irony, is mingled with the beauty. A skeleton pulls the bell on the hour at the old Town Hall while Christ and the Apostles come out to take a bow, a sight which is particularly relished by hosts of young Russian soldiers. At a shooting gallery in the Park of Culture, if you hit one spot police begin beating up a young man. In August 1987 I went looking for the vegetarian restaurant which is in a room in a block of flats on Celetna Street. First time I went, there was a sign saying it was only open for lunch. Second time there was a sign saying it was closed for the weekend. A young man with a crew cut and a wispy expression slipped out of the door and swiftly disappeared down the stairs. Third time there was a sign saying it was shut for six weeks. This time the restaurant was proclaimed on the street outside and there was a long queue stretching up the stairs. But most people turned out to be eating sausages and pork. Someone had scrawled Franz Kafka's name as an occupant of the house.

Kafka is buried with his parents at the new Jewish cemetery opposite Zelivsheho metro. The cemetery is a soothing woodland of chestnut trees and rhododendron bushes. The old Jewish cemetery in the old part of the city, with its twenty thousand gravestones, is the most stunning experience in Prague, the almost mauve gravestones very often linked by cobwebs. Near by is a museum where you can see paintings by the children of Terezin concentration camp; a butterfly, a black terrier, a ruby devil, then hangings, a coffin. At any moment you can break from these paintings and look out of the window into the cemetery which, with its green and red benches, its alder trees, is an island, a haven, a lulling miasma of lustre and shade.

Prague is a city of parks. Crossing Mánseúv Bridge just up from the cemetery you come on the gate to the sublime Wallenstein Gardens on Letenska Street. There a file of knights marched in a theatrical display to 'It's a long way to Tipperary', under the blushing frescos of Zeus and Aeneas, just before I left Prague. The subsequent walk to the Church of Our Lady Victorious, which is the home of the Child Jesus of Prague, and to the mesmeric riverside green beyond makes the places of interest along the way, the castle, the Sternberk Palace, St Vitus's Cathedral, Loreto, almost incidental.

Music, as well as verdure, is everywhere. Early evening a jazz trio starts up 'La Paloma' in the café of the Grand Hotel on Wenceslas Square. Another jazz trio plays 'La Mer' in Kavarna Slavia as boys in floral bermudas, as if in rhythm with it, skate over Máje Bridge outside. Gypsies – women in dresses patterned by peonies, men in dashingly striped trousers – gaze at sweating Dixieland bands thumping out 'Bleeker Street Parade' in the Park of Culture. While I stayed at the Meteor I could walk in the evenings to hear Shostakovich, Janáček, Schubert at the Convent of St Agnes, taking a stroll in the garden enclosure during the break. At Reduta on Narodni Street, roses in Coca Cola bottles, a mosaic of famous jazz faces among the patterns of splattered notes of music on the wall, the audience is an attentive gallery of faces, young, middle-aged, old, all veered, almost reverentially, towards the players.

It was in one of the buffets on Wenceslas Square, dog roses on the metal tables, the place crowded with women in lemon socks or old men with badges representing eagles or turkeys, that I met a punk who asked me, as a foreigner, to sponsor him for a one-day trip to West Berlin to hear Stray Cats. As I was signing the relevant document in the bank, vouching that I'd given him the necessary ten dollars for the trip, six more punks, boys and girls, turned up from nowhere and asked me to sign the same form for them. They didn't abandon me when I'd done what they wanted but accompanied me on tram Number 17 down the river to Padoli Stadion where we spent the afternoon swimming, long queues of swimmers for frankfurters and mustard, a huge, boiling sauna alongside the pool where people sat in the near-lemon light, silently, almost ceremoniously, oblivious to the sunshine outside.

At evening those punks hang around the end of Wenceslas Square. The museum at the top is radiant, the square itself powdered with colours of beds of flowers. Later red roses are given by random members of the audience to players at the Convent of St Agnes. The trio at Kavarna Slavia end the evening with 'Auld Lang Syne', while a man with the unfortunate name of Victor Sodoma mimes 'I just called to say I love you' at the Tatran Hotel, pixie-dresssed girls cavorting about him, a sign outside the hotel telling you 'a pleasant surprise is expecting you'.

One evening I met two boys singing a Banchieri duet by the

river. They were celebrating the completion of their examinations. Late at night, all over Prague, trickles of tourists from the GDR queue at windows for waffles.

Strolling with a woman when I'd lost my way by the Belvedere Gardens (closed for the moment and patrolled by a soldier with an Alsatian) I remarked on the loveliness of Prague. 'Everything is lovely for a while,' she said sadly and that comment seemed to catch the spirit of this city, a city where I saw a Dalmatian having a mock fight with a swan day after day, where groups of children go each day to a cinema in the Park of Culture to watch Carole Lombard and Mary Pickford films.

A scribe of the Jewish quarter wrote about the castle outside Prague where the Danish astronomer Tycho Brahe resided: 'And I the writer was there thrice, always for five consecutive days and saw the wonderful things, not only with the planets but also with the fixed stars.' Despite the testiness of some of its waiters, despite waitresses who hide behind grand pianos rather than serve old American couples, this city, like that view of the night sky through a sixteenth-century telescope, has a host of wonders, is a place especially for those bruised of spirit, whose faith in the loveliness of everyday things has been temporarily shattered.

Appleby-in-Westmorland

'They come out of habit, like their grandparents and great grandparents,' an old farmer from Penrith, who'd been coming to the Appleby Horse Fair all his life, told me. 'The young people come to court. They're scattered throughout the four corners of Britain the rest of the year and Appleby is the only place where they can meet up.' Perhaps he was thinking of gypsies and travellers long ago because the gypsy and travelling youths on Gallows Hill outside Appleby now don't look constricted, dressed in Hawaiian shirts, the girls in frilly flamenco skirts, often their midriffs bare, dresses emblazoned in silver, over-weening plate earrings. On the evening of 11 June, St Barnabas's Day – 'Barnaby Bright, the longest day and the shortest night' – Gallows Hill beside the Roman road, where the last execution took place in 1828, was a city to itself; modern, dashing, silver caravans, yes, but also the bow-topped Leeds wagons, the rectangular Reading wagons, the ornate Bill Wright's pot carts. Painted bouquets of cornflowers and pansies on some of them. Arabesques of gold on a liquorice background. A recurrent motif of golden nightingales, golden, joyous horses, black grapes. Then, among all this flamboyance, a sudden plain aquamarine vardo.

Cages with blue budgies, cinnamon canaries in them placed above caravans. Clusters of pansies in urns at caravan doors. A ghetto blaster on a 1975 van for sale united the entire scene in one song:

> Although I'm many miles away
> I still can hear my sweetheart say

'You're as welcome as the flowers in May
And I love you in the same old way.'

'You don't have an ounce of Lee blood in you, Nathan,' one
man, with a daintily knotted kerchief around his neck, accused
another. The name Lee was apparently competitive, fortune-
telling Lees advertised everywhere. A Kathleen Lee, an Anna-
belle Lee. A Gypsy Lee from Blackpool, one from South Wales. A
Lee whose sign declared her great-aunt had informed Lady
Bowes Lyon she'd become the Queen of England. I had my
fortune told by Gypsy Rose Mary Lee. 'You've been to America
and will be going back soon.' I was due to go to Alabama shortly.

A woman with face dark as blackened bananas emerged from a
Reading wagon to stand against the sunset; a boy, against
virtually the same stage of sunset, crawled around on his
hunkers in pursuit of a goat and its kid; a boy admired the ring of
a girl in a frilly flamenco skirt, holding her finger.

At the bottom of Boroughgate, the main street in Appleby,
young evangelists from local villages had ensnared a few Roma-
nies with renditions of hymns like 'The Old Rugged Cross'.
There was a notice on the front of one of the vardos on Gallows
Hill saying: 'I have decided to follow Jesus.' There's going to be a
conference in Airdrie, beginning 27 July, for travellers who've
found the 'truth of Jesus' and a similar, more global one
beginning 3 August in Amsterdam.

Very often gypsy women withhold baptism from their children until they get to Appleby and then have it performed, either
in St Lawrence's Church or in Appleby Catholic Church under
the sanction of the wooden Lady of Appleby, her child beside her
and she dressed in blue and mulberry, the happy portent of an
apple in her right hand.

I had arrived in Appleby on the Settle–Carlisle train, coming
through womblike valleys, dramatic river-shapes of rocks on the
hills, white hawthorn always growing in scintillating isolation,
boarded-up houses suddenly thrust up at intimate distances to
the railway line. Eric Tracey, Bishop of Wakefield, a famous
pastor to railwaymen in Liverpool, dropped dead while photo-

graphing a steam train on Appleby platform in May 1978, just before the fair.

There is an almost lavender glow from the red sandstone houses on Appleby's slanted main street, lime trees lining it, bloomers of leaves at their base. One house is not made of red sandstone. It is called the White House, perhaps because many of George Washington's relatives went to school in Appleby. John Robinson, secretary to the Lord Treasurer for some years at the end of the eighteenth century, lived here. The expression 'Before you can say Jack Robinson' comes from his antics in parliament. At the top of the street, the south of it, stands a Norman castle, in whose grounds, among the many examples of rare breeds and species, is a collection of disabled owls and a particularly lavishly bedecked peacock who keeps hissing and brandishing her feathers at entrapped pheasant fowl and salmon favorelles. The distance between the cross at the top of the street and that at the bottom was once a distance of punishments, men and women whipped between the posts.

To begin with a Danish settlement, Appleby was burned twice in the Borders wars. It was the strongly royalist Lady Anne Clifford who restored this 'poor village with a ruinous castle', creating the beautiful enclave of widows' houses off the main street, defying the Commonwealth to give special attention to the Norman church of St Lawrence. Perhaps because of the success of her work with the church Carlisle Cathedral gave its organ to St Lawrence's in 1684. In mid-Victorian times it was moved from the west end of the church to the east end, some of the pipes cut to fit under a lower ceiling. The floods of 1968 partly ravaged the organ and in 1976 it was renovated by Nicholsons of Malvern, aluminium pipes placed above the metallic grey ones to restore them to their original height, put back in its original position, this time on an eighteen-inch plinth, the first recital to mark the cultural redress given with aplomb, by all accounts, by Francis Jackson, organist to York Minster. On 12 June 1989 the church clock was stopped, the six bells with their ancient Whitechapel peal, which have been giving trouble, being sent back to Whitechapel to be recast.

From the bell tower of the church, when Appleby was county town of Westmorland, the vicar who was also mayor used to spy with a telescope, during Fair Week, to help the police. Now that Appleby is part of Cumbria (although officially it retains Westmorland in its name) there is a different style of vigilance, police coming from all over the country, from as far away as Whitehaven and Kendal.

An Irish traveller from Wolverhampton suggested to me that the powerful police presence was due to the fact that two famous traveller boxers had planned to take part in an illegal fist fight. Large sums of money would be involved by way of gambling, but gambling there would be anyway, games of 'spinning' outside the Grapes Inn by the river Eden, a seventeen-year-old boy said to have collected £6000 under his jersey this way, coins tossed in the air, heads or tails supported. If the games by the river were eventually stopped, they continued all over Gallows Hill.

In the days when the vicar was mayor, in the early 1970s, horses were raced up Boroughgate. Further back, thirty years ago, the gypsies used to camp on the roadsides leading into Appleby, coal smoke coming from the caravans, creating an industrial-type smog over the hawthorn trees and the corn chamomile.

But traditions continue defiantly. On the morning of 13 June horses were taken on a little circuit, through the shoulder-deep part of the river, under the bridge; a gypsy in bermudas enthroned on a strawberry roan mare for the ritual. A little boy chased a skewbald pony by the river edge, squirting him with Jeyes Fluid. Fairy Liquid and Jeyes Fluid were used to shampoo after the saunter through the water. Some heavily tattooed skinheads, after having gone for a swim themselves, borrowed some Jeyes Fluid to lather their heads and torsos.

Later in the day, on Gallows Hill, horses that had just been sold were shod by a blacksmith in a jockey cap. A little sand-coloured old man, in an adjacent spot, his shirt off, bent an iron bar and put it back into shape again, rippling his arm muscles as a prelude to his act. 'I'm not skint. Me daddy left me six hundred thousand, but where he left it I don't know,' he declared by way of explanation for the hat placed, for some reason, beside a copy of *The Modern Woman's Home Doctor*. Staffordshire and Chelsea pottery was sold, china ensembles of Italianate gypsies. A little girl offered to sell me a tame magpie perched on her fingers, but said she'd have to wait until her father returned to decide on a true price. Three little gypsy children rode off on a Shetland gelding they'd just purchased for £200.

In the late afternoon there was harness racing in St Nicolas' Holme, the horses and chariots, with the jockeys in ambers and clarets, speeding around under a wooded hill, the bookies from Carlisle, Bishop Auckland, Dalton-in-Furness standing on milk crates, the stench of venison burgers in the air.

Already that evening, although the main trading day is not officially until the final Wednesday, much of the trading already done, vans and caravans were leaving from Gallows Hill. This city, against the azure Cumbrian mountains, however spectacular at its unpredictable zenith, was a wondrously transient one.

An Irish traveller tried to sing a song with a vaguely Republican message to some Romany ladies in the Grapes Inn. The ladies walked away. 'It's a lovely song really. But me voice is broke,' said the man by way of apology when his audience had deserted him.

But another Irish traveller, his shirt off and his expansive belly protruding, saved the day by singing a country and western number which moved everyone. 'I cry, Mister. There's something in my eye.'

'I'll race you in Woolwich,' a man told his friend as they were parting at the end of the evening.

Outside in the night there was a jack-o'-lantern flash as a gypsy man began filming his wife and children on the river bank. 'Do you think you're from the BBC?' his wife shouted as he ordered them into a stricter proximity. On Gallows Hill quieter groups still sat around fires, children reluctant to withdraw from their elders. An accordion started up with a few bars of 'Spancil Hill' and then was silent. A boy rode a long-tailed cob in the dark, high above the allyssum-draped rock gardens of Appleby-in-

Westmorland, among the caravans, the strewn-about harnesses, the alternative, makeshift gardens – the little urns of pansies.

The farmer from Penrith had told me scornfully about people who came to Gallows Hill from the Northern towns, 'travellers for a week'. Maybe these were some of the people I saw boarding a private bus for Middlesbrough the following morning.

At the Jobcentre window a group of itinerant boys were studying the advertisements for posts as plumber's mates or labourers. I thought of another line from the country and western number the previous night. 'OK, Mister. It only lasts for a while.'

Leningrad

'I firmly believe in miracles. You gave me that belief, O Leningrad,' a Leningrad poet said just after the war and on my two visits there Leningrad has struck me as having a miraculous visual quality. In January, from the Spit – the promontory – on Vasily Island, you could see figures in black picking their way over the ice on the Neva in the mysterious winter light. The soda and ice-cream parlours on Nevsky Avenue were the places to retreat for colour. Back in Leningrad on Trinity Sunday, services having been sung the night before in St Nicholas's Cathedral and in the Alexander Nevsky Monastery, the colours of Leningrad seemed to have defined themselves out of the previous, winter void – cerulean blues, powder blues, burnt siennas, Venetian reds, almond greens, Naples yellows, buttermilk shades of white. Newlyweds toasted one another with champagne around me. Sauntering fishermen clung to peonies as well as to their rods.

Flowers are an obsessive token in Leningrad. Carrying flowers in a hotel lift you will be acknowledged by flower-bearing Russian tourists and invited to their room for a vodka or Armenian cognac. Flowers are laid by newlyweds at the tomb of Peter the Great in the Peter and Paul Fortress where Leningrad began in 1703 – chamomiles, sweet williams, carnations. They pile up beside the eternal flame in the Field of Mars, life-long benevolence invoked for newlyweds. It was the centenary of the birth of the Leningrad poet Anna Akhmatova when I was there, and on that day I watched a fleet of ambulances pull up in the cemetery in Komarova outside Leningrad, where she is buried, doctors and nurses getting out to lay flowers on her grave. In the market on Kuznecny Lane, near Dostoievsky's home, the flower-sellers keep vigil by rows and rows of red roses.

In the ice-cream parlour on Nevsky Avenue, just opposite Marata Street, Peter the cat sat regardlessly under a table, as he had in January. Often these parlours have no name but they are nicknamed. The ice-cream parlour further down Nevsky Avenue, beside Zelabova Street, is called the Frog Café, perhaps because of the green festoons, green table coverings, green marble on the walls. Likewise with cafés. One unnamed one is called the Saigon because the eating conditions are cramped. A café bearing the name 'The Black Coffee' is familiarly known as the Bell because there are bells in the patterns on the walls. Café names are a kind of samizdat in Leningrad.

In January, even on trams, old people who could speak a little English, would tell you stories about the nine-hundred-day siege, many of them about the endurance of the Hermitage, the day the head of the statue of Esmeralda came off and how it was put on again after the war, how lectures on Egyptian archaeology kept going in the evenings in the Hermitage during the worst of the siege. Red carnations were strewn in the January snow in Piskariovskoye Cemetery where half a million people lie buried. Part of the miracle of Leningrad is the miracle of its imperial environs, the palaces of Tsarkoye Selo, of Pavlovsk, of Petrod-vorets, which were used as stables or hospitals during the war, the landscapes dotted with aviaries, with garden pavilions which were ravaged, these landscapes, these palaces intact now, the fountain under Petrodvorets Palace attracting a triumphant rainbow, little girls with lavish ribbons in their hair always stomping around the spot in Petrodvorets where water, if your foot hits certain cobbles, suddenly surges in the air – a handed-down imperial joke.

An old lady at the Kirov Ballet, a Leningrader who'd been living in England since she was a child, spoke about the war and the siege too, how her family jewels had been handed over in a handkerchief by a dying relative and got to another relative in Germany. She was back on a brief visit. The boy beside us in the box asked her if she'd been an aristocrat. She seemed pleased by that question. She admired the gold-draped, Tsar's box. I preferred the sky-blue, somewhat run-down exterior. Near the Kirov there was a square of rubble under St Isaac's Cathedral and the Hotel Astoria-Angleterre where the poet Esenin committed suicide. It was through such mesmeric cityscapes that one could walk for twenty-four hours in the week of the White Nights, without feeling tired.

At about two in the morning the drawbridges on the Neva went up so you were stuck for three hours on the side you happened to find yourself on. Sailors in white stood in the slightly shaded light in the middle of squares, surrounded by a mesh of canals. Songs were sung at the fountains outside the Hermitage at this time – homespun songs – songs about Perestroika, the need to escape, the adamant need to stay. You could still take a boat down the Neva at such an hour. At about four, back-street shops open to sell the first bread and milk of the day. In the morning you pass pavement booths where women cobblers hammer at shoes, bunches of laces strung up like wigs. You can pop into little shooting galleries and take a shot at a big-eared naïvely painted mouse whose eyes blaze if you hit him. A statue of Lenin beckons you into Dom Knigi, the big bookstore on Nevsky Avenue, and you can wander down seemingly endless escalators to subway stations where vases of flowers are placed under statues of appropriate heroes.

At midday there are tanks on the streets to quench the thirst of Leningraders – a barley drink called *cuvs* is poured from these tanks. Art galleries are places to make forays on again and again rather than to linger in: the Vuillards, the Bonnards of the Hermitage seem to merge with the sense of Dvortsovaya Place outside – late-nineteenth-century street scenes, family groups with the ice-cream-vendor-studded expanse. You are likely to find such vignettes as a whole train of a family in Georgian dress staring for a long time at a Victorian painting of a bird cherry tree in the Russian Museum. But in the week of White Nights everything seemed to converge on the evening when the band started up with 'I celebrate my love for you' at the Metropole where Rasputin and Nicholas II dined, when a mother and son did a Georgian dance together, hands in the air, against a gold-lamé backdrop, at Restaurant Troika on Zagorodny Street.

But of all places at evening it is the Leningrad Jazz Club on Zagorodny Street, near Restaurant Troika, which seems to capture the spirit of Leningrad, red-shaded lamps on the tables, pictures of black American jazz artists around the walls – King Oliver and his Creole Band, Billie Holiday, Ella Fitzgerald, Count Basie – Greek sailors drinking white wine in the generous light of the foyers, Elvira Trafova singing 'Sweet Georgia Brown', people dancing the samba on a small platform; some women in low-cut, black 1950s dresses, some in early 1960s pedal-pusher trousers, some men in suits, others in shorts.

To get away from this city of Volga cars and women in turban hats, this city that seems stranded in another, agreeable time, you can catch a train from Finland Station to the pine forests of Komarova where you can bathe in the copper waters of the Lake of Pikes. In autumn people will take cans to the forests and to the fields of Pscov to pick berries and mushrooms – the women in short socks, the tattooed men.

It is fashionable now among Leningraders to call their city by its old name, Petersburg. After all it's been announced on Soviet radio that Lenin didn't really want to be buried in the Kremlin but with his mother and sister. People in cafés always struggle with some literary quotation – literature like flowers is a sustaining part of everyday life. One woman tried to get words of Chekhov to communicate how Leningraders feel about life: 'Everything should be beautiful, the face, the clothes, the thoughts.'

Yet another Leningrad poet spoke of 'the pure, ship-like lines' of this city. No description could be more apt. The passing ships at night, the clearly defined passing seasons, the snatched conversations in cafés, on trams, make this city, like no other, one of the beautiful transitory against a backdrop of what has proved indestructible beauty.

Elvis Presley Highway

'I've got a picture of Elvis like that. But there's more sweat on his face in mine.' I'd been admiring a picture of Elvis Presley wearing dramatic Prussian blue, his face cinnamon coloured, in a Mississippi roadside café, when the waitress had sidled up, commenting lovingly on it. A fat man sat entranced by George Jones's version of 'From here to the door is your freedom' coming from the jukebox. I had just entered Mississippi from the state of Alabama, intending to follow the Elvis Presley Highway from Tupelo – Elvis's birthplace – to Memphis where Graceland, his home for twenty-one years, is situated.

Mississippi is green after the arid south-east, smouldering jade green, azure morning glory flowers tumbling from the roadside into the cotton fields, slithers of dark cloud over the landscape consumed by kudzu weed.

Some of the towns along the way hold a miasma of antebellum streets. Old black ladies swept up leaves with brooms. An old man in a lavender suit, a little russet chicken feather in his hat, limped down College Street in Columbus where Tennessee Williams was born. His house, still belonging to St Paul's Episcopalian Church, is lilac grey, buff, sky blue. Near by is a plaque to a lady who started Confederate Flower Day in memory of the Confederate dead on 25 April 1866. The mudguard of a car on front of me, said: 'General Lee may have surrendered but I haven't.'

An old couple had approached a woman hanging round the Presley birthplace in Tupelo when I arrived, inquiring about the site of the Battle of Tupelo. 'Don't know. It was before my time,' she answered curtly. (It had been a Union victory.) But she was able to lavish them with information about her first sight of the Presley boy, which occurred on a visit home from Illinois in the 1930s. On the kitchen wall is a picture of him, between his parents who resemble sharecroppers in disconsolate photographs of that period. 'They look tired there,' the woman said. 'They became less tired later on.' The house – a cabin really – has two rooms. Apart from the photograph on the wall there is little else besides a framed copy of Rudyard Kipling's 'If'. Elvis spent thirteen years in Tupelo where his mother slaved in a shirt factory, his father trying to farm.

Ceramic Dalmatians and homegrown watermelons were sold at a stall near by. Nearer still a woman was having a garage sale, the main item offered being vacuum cleaners. Posters advertised a concert by a gospel singer called The Spiritual Messenger of Tupelo. Gospel singers are the main source of imaginative palpitation, of imaginative arousal in Southern towns like Tupelo, whose town centres are composed of chamois-coloured and yellow-ochre buildings, whose fringes are desultory and manically uniform. Elsewhere in the South, at a gospel concert, I'd seen a fat, grey-haired black woman drag herself round the hall, a bandage on the tip of her right foot in the shape of an Arabian slipper, and some minutes later the same woman, completely transformed, in an immaculate buttercup-coloured dress, swinging and heaving and exulting on the stage, arms outstretched, singing: 'Hold on just a little bit longer. Help is on the way.'

There is an Elvis Presley pond near the birthplace, packed with ducks, an Elvis Presley church. The ducks on the pond gluttonously converged on an old lady who'd painfully walked from a wheelchair to feed them. She and her husband were touring the United States in a van. They were from California. They'd just been to Graceland. Next stop was a canyon in Arkansas. She reminded me that Elvis had started off singing with a church choir, that of the First Assembly of Christ Church. People offered me bits of information along the way, in cafés, in the Presley birthplace, accelerating a biographical collage. There was even a tea towel suspended on one café wall which read:

Can it be true –
that this Christmas when he sings
'Mama liked the roses'
(which was written for his mother
whom he loved so much)
he will be in Heaven with his Moma
singing the song to her.

One shop along the Elvis Presley Highway sold pigs' lips and pigs' feet in jars, alongside jars of candy sticks, the pigs' feet having imbued the preserving liquid with a violet colour. A multicoloured ceramic chicken posed in pedalling position on a bicycle outside a house. There were terracotta gargoyles outside a cabin called 'Point of View'. A number of times palmists' signs beckoned. Calvary was evoked outside bungalows, a triad of tall, narrow crosses, a millionaire touring the South at the moment, distributing crosses. Churches occurred every few minutes. The Alberta Church of God. The Church of Christ, established AD 33. Signs outside them warning you: 'Owning a Bible is an awful responsibility.' 'Education is easy but wisdom is hard to get.' On Elvis Presley Boulevard, leading into Memphis which is just over the border in Tennessee, Moonies sold red roses to motorists.

Graceland, halfway down Elvis Presley Boulevard, is reached by a shuttle service from an airport-type mêlée of souvenir shops, ticket kiosks, very functional ice-cream parlours on the other side of the road. Two of Elvis's planes, stationary on tarmac, lined within by apple green and rose pink and holding enclaves of shirts with igniting, night-sky patterns, contribute to the airport atmosphere.

Elvis Presley lookalikes, looking as if they had nowhere else to go, slumped about the day I was there, one with rumpled hair, scarlet shirt, pale blue suede shoes with citron-yellow laces. Three ladies with ash-colour eruptions of hair at the back determinedly patrolled the area. But Graceland on the other side of the road, amid slightly rolling parkland, right down to the quality of the light through Tiffany glass, had the opulence and serenity of mosques in remote Arabia.

The woman who'd been hanging around the Presley birth-place in Tupelo had told me that Elvis had Graceland built for his mother, Gladys Love Presley, in 1956 but he was drafted into the army before they could settle in properly. She joined him in Fort Hood in Texas but on the way back to Graceland in 1958 she became ill and instead of being taken to Graceland from the train station in Memphis she was rushed to the Baptist Hospital in Memphis where she died.

The first thing I noticed was the quantity of ceramic monkeys among the ripples of turquoise fabric, among the burgundy lampshades. Elvis apparently had a pet chimpanzee, whom he dressed in a sailor suit, who used to pull obsessively at girls' dresses. In many of the rooms Elvis spoke to you, one way or another. In a TV interview constantly being shown in one room he was asked, after his return from the army in Germany, what his advice to young people about to serve would be. His voluptuary's lips brazenly contorted. His militarily coiffured frame shuddered a little. His head experienced a quaking resonance at the question. 'You can't fight them. They never lost yet.' Elsewhere, beside a Jewish chai pendant which he wore at his final concerts, is an inscription: 'Don't criticize what you don't understand, son, you never walked in that man's shoes.' His wife's volcanic wedding headdress near by. A poster for *Change of Habit* in which he starred with Mary Tyler Moore. 'Could she forsake her vows and follow her heart?'

Outside, among the cockscombs and the caladiums, are the Presley graves. A teddybear in a skirt beside Elvis's grave. A pool of water in the 'o' of his middle name, Aaron. His mother, Gladys, and his grandmother, Minnie Mae Presley, buried alongside him. Behind them, set in a wall, a row of primitive, ruddy-coloured, Spanish stained-glass windows. A pool near the graves with viridian lighting effects in its depths. Elvis died on 16 August 1977 after having played 'Blue Eyes Crying in the Rain' and 'Unchained Melody' on a gold-plated piano. Beside his grave are the words: 'God saw that he needed some rest and called his son to be with him.' A girl I'd met in a library in Alabama told me how her brother used to deliver Cadillacs to

Graceland. Elvis gave Cadillacs as gifts. And with each delivery he joined Elvis to sing gospel songs. Only the men sang gospel at Graceland. The girls decorated the house or brought refreshments.

In the works of William Faulkner Memphis is a city where 'Sonny Boy' is sung at funerals and ginger ale and punch served, where special beds are constructed at brothels for gargantuan customers. 'So this is Memphis. Where have I been all my life?' declares one character who's from just down the road in Mississippi.

The night I was there, 16 September, a helicopter threw fireworks in the shape of a spade from the sky to inaugurate the construction of the biggest pyramid in the world beside the Mississipi. The atmosphere on Beale Street was Dionysian. But maybe it is every Saturday night.

William Faulkner's Mississippi fraternity boys came to Beale Street and its environs to lose their virginity, to encounter madames with names like Reba Rivers. The street musician on Beale Street who drew the biggest crowd on the night of 16 September was an old black man with olive hair, who wore an ivory-yellow patterned shirt, his voice having the disconsolate, railroad whine Beale Street blues are famous for.

'I've been practising a long time now,' he told the crowd. 'So I might improve soon.'

'I'm the real Uncle Ben. Not the one on the rice packet. I have nieces and nephews all over America.'

The quips worked him up to another song: 'If I don't see you tomorrow I'll see you the next day right around noon.'

A little black boy came up and dropped a dollar in his hat.

'I'll dance at your wedding,' he shouted after the boy.

Motels are easy to get in Memphis. I got one downtown, among the yellow and rose warehouse buildings, Sun Records where Elvis made his first recordings just across the road.

In Memphis there's a 1970s soul singer who's made the transition to preacher – Reverend Al Green – and everyone is welcome to his services in the Full Gospel Tabernacle Church on Hale Road, off the Elvis Presley Boulevard, each Sunday morning. These services are joyful. A line of about twenty deaconesses clicked their fingers as they swung and jived into the church from the back, the morning I attended. They wore surplices with funnelled, half scarlet, half white sleeves. There were scarlet crosses on their stoles. To start the service a bespectacled, partly crippled boy got up and sang: 'This little light of mine, I'm going to make it shine.' Al Green, in an ultramarine gown, took up his seat at the front of the congregation. Visitors were asked to stand and say where they were from. There were three hesitant young people from Chiswick. The highlights of that service were Reverend Al Green's daughter giving a dramatic recitation and a girl, Denise, in a violet, handkerchief-hemmed top singing her story about being saved from her life of prostitution by the grace of God. Reverend Green's daughter in a white poodle dress, wearing large glasses, stomped around the altar, attesting:

> I may not have any royal blood coursing in my veins
> My name doesn't belong to any great family tree
> My living conditions are kind of down
> But I'm still determined to be
> Somebody
> Someday.

At the back of the church is a picture of planes crashing into skyscrapers, cars crashing on highways, but figures in white sheets rising from the crashes, through the windows of mulberry and vermilion skyscrapers, from Peaceful View Cemetery. There was the glitter of *diamanté* and Venetian glass throughout the church. One dress was white and pink rococo, like a candy-stick bar. Pearl necklaces were tied in fist-like knots on women's bosoms. One woman, in a black coat, waving a rose handkerchief from joy throughout the service, wore a papal dome of a hat, radiating with silver incrustations.

'If you stop condemning you might see something beautiful,' Al Green half sang as part of his sermon.

At the end, a little black girl having snuggled in my arms, we, the visitors, were told to come back. But here, as in many places in the South, you must respect and you must be prepared to give something, an anecdote, a little bit of autobiography, a description of an intersection in Catford or Forest Hill.

On my way back south, diverging just a little from Route 78, the Elvis Presley Highway, I passed through William Faulkner's town, Oxford, Mississippi. Cows half submerged themselves in lakes around Oxford. I passed a mule-drawn covered wagon. Earlier, just before Oxford, I'd seen a poster advertising a Beautiful Mule competition. Revival meetings were held in marquees towards evening, the marquees lighted up beside the cotton fields, flaps open on to the night. The congregations at these were all white for some reason and I heard a pop song coming from one – 'This will be the last time.' The moon was coral pink, low over the fields.

Back in Tupelo I stopped for a few minutes on the site of the Battle of Tupelo, two cannons on it, and again heard music coming from the night, not Elvis, not gospel, but a Tammy Wynette number, 'Golden Ring', which was mellifluous in this spot where the Confederates and the Union clashed, the Union winning, the bruised feeling of the past still in the air, as it is in so much of the South.

I got a motel in Columbus and read, in magazines picked up in the foyer, about the imminent canonization of Princess Grace of Monaco, of how it's been confirmed that Wild Bill Hickock was gay, before going to sleep.

In the morning I saw that the wall opposite the motel had a 1930s fresco on it, a sea scene, a shoe-salvage shop tucked into the building, and an old black lady, acrobatic contortions on the wings of her glasses, walking, very erect, past a sign which said 'Heaven will make it all OK.'

1990

New Orleans in autumn

'What are you going to do now?' a friend of mine in the Deep South who had suffered a great tragedy was asked.

'Go to New Orleans,' she said.

It sounded like a famous Southern line: 'Why I'll go home to Tara tomorrow.'

I've journeyed to New Orleans by Greyhound bus, by train, by car. The first time, December 1987, by bus; last autumn, living in the Deep South, I frequently made my way there by train and by car.

Going into New Orleans the first time, at early morning, by bus, manic conundrum of flyovers above dream-time esplanades of Gothic houses and still, in December, pristine gardens, I incongruously thought of lines by the ragtime poet and turbulent nomad Hart Crane: 'Remember the lavender lilies of that dawn, their ribbon miles beside the railroad ties as one nears New Orleans.' That time I stayed at a cheap, high-rise hotel at Lee Circle. 'You know why General Lee is facing north?' a loaded bag lady had cackled to me as I entered the building, referring to the bronze statue of the Confederate leader on a pedestal in the middle of the Circle. 'Because he didn't dare turn his back on a Yankee.' I suppose she thought I was a Yankee.

Later that morning I strolled from Lee Circle to the French Quarter, a boy in a sleeveless vest with an outlandish gargoyle tattooed on his arm frantically darting out of a plumbago-flanked pub and, eyes protected by dark glasses, dashing across the street to another pub; a chorus of toy white cats in low-cut, claret, strapless dresses in the window of a cat shop on Royal Street; the voice of Elton John ricocheting from one shop sound system to another, through what Hart Crane described as 'the unspeakable mellowness' of the French Quarter, past vistas of shot gun – one-room-looking – houses, lamenting doomed American love with 'Candle in the Wind'. On Dauphine Street was a bumper sticker saying: 'You have conquered, O Galileean.'

I was tentative with the city then. Last autumn, living in the Deep South made me braver. New Orleans was a place to go on Friday evenings. By car, a journey on roads lined, in autumn and early winter, by snow-in-summer blossom, the landscapes runny, horse-drawn dog-wagons trekking through them, bearing pointers and setters for the hunt, men selling milk from carts, ancestral steamboat-Gothic mansions, often a kind of febrile crab-colour, squeezed into the distance.

By train it was usually a journey with revellers for company. A man who'd just got out of Atlanta State Penitentiary, going to New Orleans to continue what he'd been doing for eight years in gaol, writing poetry and reading the Bible. Once, as we crossed Lake Pontchartain by train, winter darkness crowding in, a man leaned over and told me: 'I'll marry the first woman who says, when I invite her to dinner, "Let's eat at McDonald's". She'll be a money saver.'

Many people in New Orleans are ashamed of the French Quarter and will try to lead you uptown in the evenings, to Pascal Manales on Napoleon Street where you have to wait among a sentimental fresco of photographs of Perry Como, Jack Dempsey, Renato Scotto before eating, to music clubs like Tyler's on Magazine Street where desultory college students mill, to Cajun restaurants beside suburban cemeteries, statues of Confederate soldiers, Civil War nurses, brothel madames who became respectable, looking in at you as you eat.

But it's the quarter I was first drawn to and love, the courtyards strung with coral vine and bougainvillaea; the ponds of cerulean water outside back windows; the raised Louisiana cottages with asparagus fern hanging from their porch roofs; an entire avenue of weeping figs; the house colours – wistaria blue, sunset peach, Pompeiian red.

At night the place is rabid with tourists but tourists reinforce the individuality of the performers – the old lady with the chignon hair-style at La Fitte's on Bourbon Street who plays the piano and sings: 'I hate to see that evening sun go down'; the strippers, male and female, in a club on Bourbon Street who never discard their G-strings – 'We all have kids. That's why we do it,' a girl in a top hat and tails told me; a woman in a tomato-coloured coat-dress, beefy earrings on her, dancing with a woman in a leopardskin coat in the Bombay Club on Dumaine Street under pictures of Winston Churchill, faded British horsemen in the shade of peepul trees, and statuesque old Indian men in voluminous dhotis; the old black man with almost indigo-blue skin, his bass viol held aside, not so much singing as whispering 'Please Release Me', making it something antiphonal for the ladies from Boston or Charlotte, North Carolina, crouched on the floor in Preservation Hall on Peter Street. The old lady at La Fitte's frequently sings 'Non, je ne regrette rien' too which reminds me of the story of the first battalion of French girls sent here in 1721, from a house of correction. A midwife called Madame San Regrets was sent after them.

On an overcast Saturday afternoon at what seemed like the end of autumn last year, the very end of November (there was to be, uniquely, a fall of snow in December, a month when, in Tennessee Williams stories, the fugitive kind are still getting the sun on Canal Street), I began a very conscious journey through New Orleans, to redefine what I knew about the city and the area. I didn't want my memory of the city to be blurred.

I started at the Voodoo Museum on Dumaines Street which is also a place where voodoo rituals are enacted, an altar there, an empty bottle of Mateus Rosé on it, a bulb of garlic, some cent coins, a ribaldly laughing buddha; above it photographs of people who had taken part in the rituals and who looked happily rewarded by them – marines, very ordinary-looking middle-aged couples.

Before I left I saw fresh-looking chicken feathers on the floor.

From the museum I went to the Church of Our Lady of Guadalupe on North Rampart Street, a church which is crowded with statues of saints, St Barbara, St Expeditus, St Teresa, St

Clara, Blessed Martin, St Jude Thaddeus, much of their clothing carob-coloured, penitential-coloured.

These are also voodoo saints, people coming to kneel in trances before them, praying Catholic or voodoo prayers. St Expeditus is a Roman soldier. He came to New Orleans in a crate long ago – no one knew his name. On the box was the word 'Expedite'. So they called him St Expeditus. There is a picture of Our Lady of Perpetual Help over an altar. You see pictures of Our Lady all over New Orleans; Our Lady of Guadalupe above the jumbo shrimps at the French market.

Near the Church of Our Lady of Guadalupe is St Louis Number 1 Cemetery where Marie Laveau, the Pope of Voodoo, is buried. She was a hairdresser before she became a voodoo priestess. From her rituals jazz started – so they told me at the Voodoo Museum – African drums used with European wind instruments on Congo Square on Sunday afternoons. There were crosses scratched all over her tomb. Her name, Marie Glapion Laveau, on it. The Spanish handed over New Orleans to the French in her childhood and then the French sold it to America. She saw molasses running in the gutters of New Orleans when the city fell to the Union and she lived to see grandeur fade and hear the first sounds of jazz in the air.

The Projects overlook the cemetery – a block of cheap housing. You are warned before going into the cemetery that you may be mugged for your Air Jordans – high-soled boots, 'the limousines of boots' – but everyone around the Projects was benign to me. Charity Hospital, which was on my way uptown, has had its beds reduced from 3,000 to 500. Hundreds of people crowd in there each day for attention and wait for hours under wall paintings of rainbow-illustrated flower stalls. But among the set grimness of poverty in New Orleans are street cars decorated with garlands of pine from early November on; a sketch of a woman with spidery hair on lavender paper by a grave in St Louis Number I; yellow powder spilt from a gris-gris bag – voodoo bag – on the steps of a multi-galleried, violet-coloured house on North Rampart Street.

And not far from the Projects are Fairlands Racing Grounds

where, on Saturday afternoons, people sit in inner halls as though they're waiting for a Greyhound bus, watching, on video screens, egrets take flight on the racing track as the horses take off, the place a thriftstore fashion display of flared trousers, wide, damascened ties, the odd, ingenuous pair of spectator pumps from another age, a more exotic thriftstore.

I went up Joseph Street, parallel to St Charles Avenue, on my way out of the city. Hebrew Number 3 Cemetery is here. I have a friend who is a black musician in New Orleans and last year he took part in a jazz funeral for a Jewish musician. There was a bit of a tiff with the rabbi because the songs were – by their nature – non-Jewish. But a cultural compromise was quickly arrived at and the funeral went on, the rabbi leading the little parade, the musicians joyfully delivering 'In the sweet by and by we will meet on the beautiful shore' and a Hebrew love-song someone remembered from the Korean War: *'Beimir Beistdu Schön'*.

A street with little famished-looking bars – Tchoupitoulas – then on a street corner Tipitinas which was Professor Longhair's favourite venue for years and where there are jazz concerts given by children each Sunday afternoon – slide trombones, clarinets, and slither versions of 'Autumn Leaves' by six-year-old girls. Later on Sundays a Cajun dance is held here – scores and scores of people jitterbugging and waltzing to rampant accordions and wailing fiddles. The Cajuns were French settlers who lived in Acacia in Nova Scotia. They were expelled by decree of the English king in 1755 and made their way to the bayous around New Orleans, a landscape of swamps, trickled by cedar knees protruding from the water. Henry Wadsworth Longfellow wrote the poem 'Evangeline' about his exodus, about this 'ship-wrecked nation'.

I'd spent Thanksgiving with a Cajun family near Plaquemines, in a house surrounded by hackberry trees and pecan trees, the late-afternoon light picking up labyrinths of water in the meadows around the house. There was a photograph on the wall of a bride dancing, dollar bills pinned to her fleur-de-lys-patterned gown and a statue of Our Lady of the Assumption, patroness of Cajuns, in the background. The son of the family had turned

Calvinist and he said grace. In the distance discreet little flames were coming out of the Heaven-soaring tower of a chemical factory.

On Saturday mornings in Fred's Lounge in Mamou, near Baton Rouge, there is a massive Cajun dance, gangly men in gym gear, red kerchiefs round their heads, taking wild steps to music which seems to recreate exodus, entry by boat and raft into this land of 'Spanish moss and mystic mistletoe'.

On the outskirts of New Orleans, on my Saturday afternoon drive through the city, I watched the chital deer in Aubudon Park – clove-coloured deer splashed by white spots – but on my way to City Park I came across a school fête, Ellis Marsalis, the father of ʲ the trumpeter Wynton Marsalis, playing a piano under a small floodlight as it was already dark. After him there was a samba band and the parents, children and musicians joined in a samba, snaking out of the yard and disappearing down a street where dogs were barking, some of the last people to disappear being two women in creole dress, luxuriant sage-coloured feathers on their heads; a man with a lambchop beard, in a waistcoat, who told me he'd been playing a plantation owner from Tipperary who'd helped Andrew Jackson in the Battle of New Orleans in 1815. The school yard was empty for the moment, save for a few women in military anoraks who were selling gris-gris bags to aid this Montessori school.

I gave up the idea of proceeding to City Park, returned to my hotel, the de la Poste on Chartres Street. It was a hotel recommended by a friend from Alabama. There'd been a time she'd stayed in grander hotels in New Orleans, with an ancient and dignified aunt. Once, in the early 1960s, this aunt ventured to the hotel cabaret. Red Fox was the artiste. She'd never heard such language before – 'I have twenty-three whores in New York City' – and she went to the ladies' room where she passed out. It was the last of the grand hotels in New Orleans for my friend.

'America's two biggest problems at the moment are drugs and bad syntax,' a Jewish lady with multicoloured bugle-beads sewn into her sweater told me at Café du Monde that evening. I didn't stay in the Quarter that particular evening but went uptown, past sidewalks where youths advertised the fact they were selling cocaine – white lady – or crack by standing on litter wagons. I was going to a black music club, the Winnah's Circle, on St Bernard Street. My companion and I were the only two white people there. A boy I got talking to about the horror, the desecration of drugs, told me, 'I go out for a few drinks and fun but I always go and have a few words with the Lord first.' The band, which included a violinist, had just played Concierto de Aranjuez. I knew I was in an area where Air Jordans slung over electric wires passed on some message about drug dealing but I was not scared.

Nothing about this city ultimately frightened me. Because, for all its supposed dangers, it is also a city of talismans – bottles of holy oil sold at the Church of Our Lady of Guadalupe; benevolent crosses piled up on the tomb of Marie Laveau; a bumper sticker saying: 'Even the loneliest river runs somewhere safe to sea.'

Harry Crosby, Hart Crane's flamboyant American-in-Paris publisher and equally impulsive traveller, said: 'In America one never becomes part of a church. At Chartres one becomes part of the Cathedral.' St Louis Cathedral on Jackson Square, ironically at the end of Chartres Street, with the bonny blue Confederate flag inside, its slate-colour, hexagonal spires, two of them topped by pelicans, must be an exception.

On the Sunday morning after my late night at the Winnah's Circle, as mass was going on inside, a little black boy, in a crocheted, lemon and navy spangled jersey, did some hambone dancing outside. All the time, as he clattered with his steel-capped shoes, chanting a refrain which would have been approved by Crane and all the other voyagers who experience New Orleands's rainbow mesh:

> Hambone, Hambone, where you been?
> Round the world and am going again.

South African diary

Softly, tenderly Jesus is calling
Calling for you and for me
Safe on the portals
He's waiting and watching
Watching for you and for me.
Come home to me.
You who are weary come home.

9 September 1990. The third-class carriage coming in from Simonstown. A town of magnolia-coloured porticoes, the feet of the pillars slashed with Wedgwood blue or vermilion stripes; advertisements all over windows for batteries, pies and cocktail olives. One old advertisement for Durex. It features a man in a polo neck and a woman with bouffant hair-style. 'Plan your family carefully.' Suddenly, at a stop, a black man in a tawny and crimson striped tie, leaps on the train and starts playing an accordion and singing in Afrikaans: 'Kom Volg Jesus.' 'Come follow Jesus.' He is followed by three women, one with lime and yellow striped rattles which she plays vociferously. One with a tambourine. The last, in a soot-black coat, who begins to dance around the carriage, bowing her head. After their number a little girl with her hair in tight corn rows, who wears green, yellow, black – the colours of the ANC – and the crimson lake of revolution, gives us a song.

Ride on Moses.
Ride on King Emmanuel.
He is the golden son.
He is the king who will save the world.

It's dusk outside but the sun will be going down on the western side of the Cape. I am back in Alabama, exactly a year ago. A gospel-song concert in a cinema where I was, like now, the only white person.

Little girls in white party dresses, pearl contraptions hanging from their corn rows, dog-rose taffeta around their ankles. Women in cocktail hats, in *décolleté* dresses, in dresses with plunging backs. Men in sharkskin suits. The man on the stage, doubled up almost against the hand-held microphone, is telling how he was crippled as a baby, how his mother prayed over him like Daniel prayed in the lions' den – of his subsequent cure.

Hands are raised in trance-like testimonial. A woman stands up. Tinsel stars are twinkling on the ceiling. 'This man is the son of God,' she cries. Another woman starts rolling on the floor between the rich crimson seats.

Outside, during a break, after the song: 'Don't know where I'll be. On the roadside or at my door. But, Lord, I hope you'll be there', under a poster for *Brigadoon*, a woman had proposed to me. 'Are you married? I'd like to marry again.'

Now the man on stage starts talking about white men who'd have them scrub floors if they got a chance, descends from the stage and, microphone still in his hand, starts advancing towards me. I make a dash for it, get on my bicycle outside and speed up the street, past a technicoloured advertisement for pancakes and strawberry sauce in Woolworths' window.

In South Africa I stand my ground.

Soweto, September 1990. On Masopha Street a woman in the fuchsine garb of the Shangan tribe suddenly looks around towards the taxi. There's a huge Omo packet as advertisement against the sky. A dry cleaner's in a caravan, the caravan penned in by grazing oxen. Outside a hostel where about twenty men sleep to one room a woman sits over an array of second-hand shoes which she's selling, a little stove keeping her warm. After five years of a rent strike there's rubbish everywhere, rubbish burning sacrificially in skips. But nothing about the worst of

Soweto – Mshenguville shanty town – is as bad as the shanty towns I saw in Port Elizabeth. Kleinskool – the coloured shanty town. Kwazekela – the black shanty town. Corrugated iron, plastic, even posters of Maxi Priest making up home. One isolated pump for water. A turquoise-hued fast-food joint beside one section of a shanty town. Elsewhere in the black and coloured areas of Port Elizabeth the houses are neat – flamingo pink, nursery blue – a tapestry showing a bulldog playing snooker, a spaniel in a bowler hat just behind him inside one one-roomed house. In the shops huge sausage shapes of peanuts hang and some buildings are burnt out after the riots of the second week in August, some buildings just singed. Outside a teacher training college, students hitch into the white centre of town – a town of alabaster fan-shape-topped buildings, coffee-coloured Doric pillars, surly-looking mock Queen Anne houses.

One part of the coloured area of Port Elizabeth is called Katanga. There are kites stuck all over cables and the white authorities are thinking of putting the cables underground because people keep stealing bits of them at night. Near Katanga is the poor white area. There the whites still insist on having their black servants call them 'Boss'. The information is told to me as a joke by Peter, the hare-lipped taxi man who knows Ireland by the graffiti in North of Ireland pictures: 'In loving memory of a fallen comrade.'

19 September 1990. A rust-purple train passes through Soweto, below the even, concentration-camp rows of hostels, among the middle-class streets named after streets in Hollywood. This is a country of trains, buses; de luxe buses, first-class buses, second-class buses, third-class buses. 'Beauty's only skin deep but black is as deep as bone,' an old black man had said, talking to himself, as a bus I was on had pulled out of New Orleans a few years ago. We drove through Alabama, the man talking sonorously at the back about an epic sight he'd seen once, candle-carrying boats being blessed way out on the Caribbean. Outside the fields were golden, sepia-coloured in turn, and black people looked at us from the porches of houses where they sat or from the dog-runs

of houses where they halted in walking. By default I was back living in Alabama two years later and in turn the experience of having lived in Alabama sent me to South Africa.

Outside a plantation house in Alabama, little huts near the house, miniature chrysanthemums in orange paper-wrapped pots outside the huts, a woman had lamented to me how in her childhood the cotton fields had been a scherzo of scarlet shirts and dresses. Now the young black people had gone to Detroit. But in South Africa in September 1990 fields of neonate sorghum throbbed with colour – women in poppy-red skirts bending to pick the bad grass.

21 September 1990. The bus from Johannesburg to Cape Town. It has stopped at Bloemfontein. A little boy comes up to me with a bag. There's a birthmark charcoaled just above his lip. 'Does Uncle like children?' In South Africa, though he looks virtually white, he would have been classified as coloured until recently. A grandmother, a grandfather coloured. He has elected to be my companion for the night. At each café stop he buries his face in his hands before eating or drinking. 'Thank you, Lord, for this day you gave us and for the food on the table.' 'I am the *latlametjie* of my family,' he – Jonathan – says in Kimberly, where a black man wearing a damascened tie and a bowler hat comes to the bus looking for a daughter who has not turned up and then goes away, sits down and starts gazing, for some reason, at transparencies of X-rays. '*Latlametjie*' is the smallest. At another stop, Jonathan beside me, a black man tells me of the last time he voted, Egypt, the desert war, 1943, as if he tells this to travellers in the cold every night. There are a few white men beside him who are on the dole – '*aalmoes*' they say – and they ask for money. Each time there are soldiers outside – in rust-purple – as the bus stops briefly Jonathan looks out. He's got a cousin in the army. Like his cousin he belongs to a house church. Each Sunday morning he drinks wine in someone's home.

You're in a sand-coloured part of this country, a sulphurous yellow part and suddenly there's a religious inscription – on a lamppost, on a wall.

'If a man also lies with mankind, as he lieth with a woman,
both of them commit an abomination.' Leviticus

Above this inscription in the veldt a picture of a preacher from
Louisiana in a wide 1950s tie, a halo of light two feet over the
preacher's head. A black boy in an impeccable dark suit gets out
of a bus in the little Karoo mountains, carrying framed hardboard
with heavy dried flowers stuck on it, a Kingdom Hall of the
Jehovah's Witnesses a few feet away, buff sheep in the fields.
Inside the bus a girl soldier sleeps on a teddybear and a host of
Afrikaans women who look like elderly Doris Days – all primrose, almost albino curls, candy pink colours – yap. An owl with
a dicky bow hangs at the front of the bus and in the distance I see
two cranes beside water as the sun begins to go down, the sky
sloe-blue, gold.

'Behold, I shall create new heavens, and a new earth: and the
former shall not be remembered, nor come to mind.' Isaiah

That was beside a place where the third-class bus stopped in
Eastern Transvaal, the men getting out to urinate in a group in a
burnt flaxen field. Hawkers imploded on the bus – walking down
the aisle, selling watches they carried in buckets. One smoky-
haired boy offered me a package of silver bullets, touching my
crotch to indicate what they were for. Most of the men on this bus
wore trilbies. The women wore hats, wine-red hats, black berets.
There were Persian lilac trees – syringas – in the fields outside,
yellow wattle trees, delicate fever trees, crimson-leaved fig trees.
One young man – the whites of his eyes brandy coloured – wore
a bronze-purple officer's-style hat. On it the inscription: 'Saint
Eugena's Zion Christian Church.' He was going back to work in
the Transvaal from his home in Pretoria. He doesn't like it up
there. 'I go out for a few drinks and they throw me in gaol.'
Another man was travelling from Soweto to his farm near
Nylstroom. He grows papayas, oranges, millet, onions. Recently
a Jewish professor from an English Midlands university visited
him in Soweto, went to see the Iwisa Kaiser Chiefs, the Moroka
Swallows, the Orlando Pirates play and liked Soweto so much

after an English Midlands city – his flat was beside a showroom for luxury showers – he applied for permission to live there. But permission was refused. 'Why?' the man asked in amusement. His trilby was smashed down on his head and he wore a chocolate-brown suit, the same as the rent collector did in Ballinasloe when I was a child.

At one stop a girl, her belongings beside her in plastic food containers, sang a song in Xhosa as she waited for another bus.

'*Thina Sibambene no Sotha na amagingxi-gingxi.*'

'We are fighting the evil spirit.'

On a metropolitan bus in Port Elizabeth a few days previously, by the sea, I heard another song in Xhosa. A man in navy workman's clothes just suddenly rose and started chanting a song which called for Nelson Mandela and Dr Mangosuthu Buthelezi to meet, and then a boy on the bus who was munching a bunny chow sandwich – curried bread – joined in.

In Johannesburg a woman in a dress patterned with peonies, waiting in a half-mile long queue for a taxi to Soweto – to avoid trains – was humming another song in Xhosa and the crowds listened.

'*Ndisoloko ndiwnye no Thixo.*'

'I'm always with God.'

Behind her a porticoed shop of white and ultramarine, a banner saying: 'Bulbulios call for peace. Nothing more than ten rands.' The sunset behind the skyscrapers was peach and made a strange clash with the colours of clothes in the windows of clothes emporiums – brown, dull red, off-white; clusters and clusters of clothes, clusters and clusters of shops, clusters of boy models in windows, many in American baseball outfits, in American flaps.

In Johannesburg, this city of pearl-white skyscrapers, of chocolate-coloured clothes windows, of musky second-hand clothes, of mustard-coloured train billboards, of monkey-gland curries, of knoberries, pangas, axes, I met an Irish boy who'd left Ireland years ago, partly because he was gay, he says. He has a young friend who's dying of Aids now in Parktown Hospital. His cranium has expanded and parts of his insides are protruding.

He's from Benoni in the East Rand – a landscape where tractors sift henna earth. He came into Johannesburg, fleeing a culture which has 'I'll kick his arse' as a response to every crisis, frequenting bars like the Harrison Reef, Connections.

After I'd spoken to the Irish boy in a pizza parlour on Pretoria Street I came across a triad of old English ladies feeding wild cats outside Hillbrow Hospital. The cats were darting through a railing, between a yesterday, today and tomorrow tree – blue, white, navy – and the pavement.

'This used to be our hospital. Now we just come back for the wild cats. We couldn't see a cat go hungry.'

A black man in pointillistically dotted pyjamas, his neck bandaged, looked on.

Cape Town, 24 September 1990. On Sandy Beach I meet some-one from Ireland I last saw in the Milky Way at Kelly's Corner. He had a car accident in Dublin. Came here, via Cairo, to have plastic surgery, and stayed.

The beach is engulfed by lemon, purple, mauve vygies and pincushion proteas, by yellow-bolled knoppies, by wine tumble-weed, by turquoise turrets of mountains. A black woman is breast-feeding her child, her naked breast like one of those mountain turrets. She wears a T-shirt which shows a scene from recent South African history, Sharpeville, Soweto riots, a SADT Buffel firing on a crowd.

This man is from Cork and so is Dermot, a boy staying at the YMCA who's a gardener in Cape Town. He was born in Cork, of an Irish mother and a father from Rugby. His mother started travelling when she lived in England in the early 1960s – Club holidays. She met Dermot's father in South Africa. He wore a tattoo on his left shoulder: 'If I die in combat box me up and bring me home.' A favourite South African tattoo at the time. And he introduced her to a cocktail which was the rage in Rugby. Amoretto. Baileys. Brackish Mexican liqueur. They returned to England. Dermot was born during a holiday in Cork. But Dermot's mother found the anti-Irish racism of England too much after South Africa and they returned.

First they lived in the Eastern Transvaal where Dermot went to primary school with Irish nuns in the Rosenberg Convent. Then they moved to Cape Town where he went to a multiracial school run by Irish Christian Brothers in Greenpoint. Now his parents have returned to the Transvaal and he's stayed here, living sometimes at the YMCA, sometimes with his girlfriend.

The city his mother first came to had signs on benches saying 'Slegs Vir Blankes', 'Whites Only' among the carnelian and auburn-coloured Dutch-gabled buildings, among the serrated ultramarine of porticoed entrances, among the galleried buildings hugged by date palms. It was the buildings and the flowers that won. The flowers of Cape Town – the down-hanging moon flower with auburn ends, the richly scarlet aloe, coral and sugarbush, the pink and white azalea, the mauve and complicated tree ageratum, the orange crane flowers with cobalt tongues, the orange clivea, above all the honey-coloured Port Jackson mimosa tree. She lives now by a lake in the Transvaal, the house surrounded by kameeldoringboom trees, a tree which has creamy-grey shield-like pods standing up on the branches.

Dermot helps me to identify the trees, the flowers, the birds of South Africa; the fried-egg flower I saw in the Transvaal; the lemon Namaqualand daisies I saw coming into Cape Town with Jonathan, the deep orange calendulas, the purple lobelias; the statice I saw on graves in Soweto; the inky-centred randknuckles sold by women on Adderley Street who wear peacock-green scarves; some of the flowers I saw cycling to the Cape of Good Hope are unidentifiable, frog-coloured leaves with crimson dapples, white interwoven cauliflower shapes, but he knows the yellow weaver which flies among these flowers.

27 September 1990. I watch the sun going down over Robben Island, from Signal Hill, with Dermot. There are tugboats, freighters and a drilling ship out on the sea. Below are the high-rise buildings of Greenpoint. The sun is peach, the cirrus clouds primrose-coloured. A little swarm of young revellers in dinner suits, short silver-lamé or black dresses have come, armed with champagne, one boy's hair a cadmium blond Viking's over his

dress suit. A little battalion of schoolboys in green and canary-yellow striped school blazers suddenly appear, their feet bare. A black man is lathering his hair with shampoo on the side of the hill, using a bucket of water, as he awaits the dramatic point of the sunset. What looks like a few hundred cormorants fly low over the sea. A guinea fowl goes up to look at the people with the champagne.

I think of the people I've met in this city. A man from Beirut – 'All I know is that Mohammed was prophet and I don't care about anything else, factions, vengeance' – who remembered the lorries painted with swans in Beirut; a rabbi from West Hampstead who plays klabbejas in a Turkish baths every Saturday afternoon; an Indian woman called Dawn who started following me my first day in South Africa. She wore a two-piece dress, a slit in the ankle-length peach dress. There was a cyclamen spot on her forehead. What religion does that represent I asked her. 'All religions,' she replied contemptuously. She lives under a milkweed tree in Hout Bay. 'If apartheid ends I'll kill myself. There'll be too many love children.' As I boarded the train for Simonstown, a man in a koofekei going by behind her, she started throwing azaleas at me. 'Beauty is sorrow.'

'You can't take my richness from me. But you can murder me,' Peter, a second-hand clothes dealer from Guguletu township told me. He had a girlfriend called Letetia from Cape Town and one called Sylvia in the township. The women are hungry for men there, they far outnumber the men he says fearfully – his tie is a mark of his profession, wide, night-sky blue, a ruddy streak going through it. They surround him, touch his private parts as he walks home at night and try to abduct him to a 'jol'.

In the Malay quarter a woman in a grey velvet biretta told my fortune under a picture of a Hindu-like Sacred Heart, bird droppings all over the wall from a Ku-Klux-Klan-hooded, rosy-cheeked love bird and from a scruffy, moulting Indian dovetail, bottles of crimson potions on shelves, bubbly movements in those potions. 'Someone wants to poke you with a knife or shoot you with a gun.'

I thought of a man I'd seen in a township, his head covered by a pink balaclava, a stick in his hand, a woman cycling by him, her shopping tucked in a rug which engulfed her backside, as if he wasn't there.

'When the tension is high,' Peter the clothes dealer said of Nelson Mandela, 'he takes a puff on a cigarette and considers the situation. If there's no truth on the table you fight. But I myself am a churchman and leave all to God. Things will not be better for all tomorrow. But soon.'

The sun is suddenly an iridiscent, hard-edged boll, more and more cirrus clouds delineated in the heavens, pink, primrose-coloured. Then it disappears, the bottom of the sky a uniform, relinquished lilac. I've known Dermot for three days. I'll probably never see him again. But he has brought me to this sunset.

And when you move people do sometimes recur, by chance. I think of a boy I met in Leningrad, Christmas 1988. Six months later, on a return trip to Leningrad, I met him in the Tchaika Bar by the Griboeva Canal. In the meantime, helped by his mother, he'd slashed his wrists to avoid the army and had been put in Gatchingh Hospital with some of the mentally retarded people who he said had allowed themselves to be fucked for a cigarette. The lady doctor had told him: 'We couldn't get out. But you must.' At Anna Akhmatova's grave, on her centenary day, the Patriarch of Leningrad praying, the same boy, Sergei, asked me about Anna Akhmatova, pondering her determination to stay in Russia. 'Why commit suicide?'

Maybe some countries are worth committing suicide over. South Africa has reminded me over and over of Russia, maybe the bigness of the place, maybe the trains, a sense from the landscape, rarely felt in the British Isles, that recourse to God is always possible.

It hasn't reminded me just of the American South but the American South was there; a freak advertisement in the veldt for a preacher from the American South; the same church brands – the Moravian Church, the Apostolic Church; the same flowers – hibiscus, poinsettia, azalea. It was like taking a bus down the road from the Greyhound bus station in Alabama which had the vinyl chairs outside.

Just a closer walk with Thee.
Precious Jesus let it be.
I can never be dissatisfied
While you're walking by my side.

A secretary bird beside a small lake in the veldt, a newly green willow tree in the middle of a field, a meadow of newly sprouted lucerne grass, a black boy riding a chariot by a row of tea shacks and stopping by one which had the number 87 chalked outside; it was Alabama in the spring.

One place leads to another, one Greyhound bus journey leads to another Greyhound bus journey, a different set of characters, a different talisman by the driver's window, a different kind of courage required.

Before we leave Signal Hill I consider racism, how Dermot's mother and so many Irish people had come to this country to flee racism in England. People like the Irish woman from County Waterford in the viridian trouser suit and viridian hat I met in Fish Hoek, the whitest place in South Africa, as she sat on a bench watching the sea. Not far away I'd seen the grave of a young drowned Irish sailor. Bartholomew Maloney. Able Seaman. 1863. 'Though full of life death cometh quickly.' The woman had lived in the Woodthorpe suburb of Nottingham for a few years. Now a rich woman, like so many white South Africans, she fears nationalization. Maybe she'll be going back to County Waterford after all. There were whales out on the sea and our conversation turned to those and she got merrier the way people in South Africa get merry when they identify a bird, a flower.

Nationalization or not, rich or poor, black or white, I take one last look at the lilac horizon and I remember how you used put on the Nina Simone song 'Ain't got no' on the jukebox in the Milky Way at Kelly's Corner and a multi-coloured constellation would balance before the record played, as the smashed faces of figures in blue denim suits walked by outside.

Ain't got no mother.
Ain't got no friends.
Ain't got no love.
What have I got nobody can take away?
I've got myself.
I've got life.

Return to Ballinasloe:
a record for November 1990

It is a tradition in Ballinasloe and one that probably linked many fireside stories for centuries afterwards, that when Ballinasloe Castle was surrounded by Cromwell's men the royalist governor, Antony Brabazon, dived out of a top window in the dead of night, into the moat, and, after much fumbling around the British Isles, made his way to Spain where he died in 1654. In the chronicles of the Brabazon family, written by a Mr Hercules Sharpe and published in Paris in 1825, it is mentioned that he has a spectacular baroque tombstone in a Spanish cathedral, in keeping with the daring of his escape from Ireland, but the cathedral or the city in which it is situated are not named, by dint of clannish discretion or unyielding sense of conspiracy. When I first travelled to Spain with the sideburns and the gaucheness of the early 1970s I imagined it to be one of the elephantine stone mounds in cathedrals in jacaranda-clouded southern cities.

Ballinasloe came into being as a trading village around a ford on the river Suck between County Roscommon and County Galway. It mainly lies in County Galway – east Galway. Not just the bridge over the Suck but Ballinasloe Castle – originally the seat of the O'Kellys – mark the break on the road between Roscommon and Galway, the castle swaddled in dark ivy. You are in flat countryside where the shade of green has a clandestine feel, where tributaries of the river Suck are everywhere – messages running through the sometimes unnervingly dark countryside. In the early eighteenth century the Trench family purchased the locale from Catholic descendants of Edmund Spenser and the village became a town – big, imposing limestone houses, generously wide streets. From the middle of the eight-

eenth century to the middle of the nineteenth century the annual
horse fair was the largest in Europe. Traders frequently visited it
from Moscow.

During this year's fair English convoy people, shellshocked,
wandered through the crowded streets. They felt there was no
longer room for them in England. 'We've got the right of firing
here,' one young man in a periodically slashed, valerian-col-
oured jersey told me, holding up his ringleted boy on Church
Hill, tinkers racing traps on a track in the fair-green behind him.
'Firing' is firewood. Near by a girl from Westbury-on-Trym with
a Marie Antoinette hair-do, leather toga on her, black stockings,
played 'Rocky Road to Dublin' on a tin whistle while a youth
with lemon and scarlet laces on his boots listened.

Two billygoats escaped on the convoy people while they were
in Ballinasloe for the fair and in November the billygoats were
arriving at people's doorways, come evening, with the smell of
sausages.

In a pub on Dunlo Street, Ballinasloe, during the fair, children
were jammed on the knees of a Belfast family as they launched
into 'On the one road, carrying the one load, on the road to God
knows where' under a picture of Moscow Sportag – the Moscow
soccer team who wear blue-and-white jerseys. Was the poster a
salute to the days when horse traders came here all the way from
Moscow and stayed at Gill's Hotel?

In the fair-green, where horses weren't brushing against one
another, wellingtons were laid out and rows of second-hand
trousers. I purchased a pair of grey flannel trousers for £6 in a
blue tent where the light made it seem like a blue grotto.

We were warned, growing up, that Ballinasloe had the largest
mental hospital in Europe. The first building went up in 1833 and
extensions and additions haven't stopped since. But such knowledge doesn't deter Ballinasloe people from incessantly going
back.

The flavour of the saints depicted in its churches is exotic – St
Rose of Lima in stained glass in St Michael's Catholic Church, St
Catherine of Alexandria beside a porous-patterned tree on a wall

of the twelfth-century Clontuskert Priory four miles from Ballinasloe.

In November I came back to the town and, recreating childhood bicycle journeys, on a hired bicycle I made a tour of the
medieval monastic ruins that form an exhilarating demi-necklace
around Ballinasloe, stretching from County Galway into Offaly
where it is adjacent to Roscommon. The landscape was to a great
extent burgundy now with the wealth of rowan trees and bryony
bushes.

I started with the fourteenth-century Kilconnell Priory seven
miles west of Ballinasloe on the old Dublin–Galway road. The
O'Dalys successfully warded off Cromwell's men from it in the
1640s but by an edict of King William and Queen Mary the friars
had to leave by 3 January 1698. They dispersed to Lisbon,
Corunna, Saint-Malo, some of the longest-surviving friars in
Ireland.

Now the priory is a mysterious skeleton – a cluster of savagely
isolated gables – graves strewn among it. Honorias, Anastasias.
Marjories remembered; plastic lilies, red plastic carnations, a tiny
gold Christ on a cross – all this under glass – over a name like
Hozier. A narrative on the wall in one place telling you 'Mathyas
Barnewall Lord Barrow of Trimblestown who being transplanted
into Connaught with others by orders of the usurper Cromwell
died at Monivea'. Of a sudden you'll see a country woman, a
mourner, peering through a medieval window. Some of the
graves are recent, the date of decease of a Ballinderry farmer not
considered profane to put alongside 1667, the date of decease of
an Irish aristocrat.

Lights are lit around the head of the Virgin Mary as you enter
the village, a peach robe embracing Christ in a churchyard. Pairs
of girls link arms. The library is wedded to the bank – in the same
building. A plaque to a local MP – 'noble citizen and true patriot'
– determines the point where you step from the street on to the
priory grounds.

There was a rainbow behind the priory that day. The ruins
elevated theatrically under a sky in which low, ungainly clouds

scudded over in an orderly way. The rainbow followed me through the black bogs of Aughrim where the last decisive battle of Ireland was fought between the Williamites and the Jacobites almost exactly three hundred years ago, in 1691. It followed me past splendidly gabled country houses and isolated oaks to Clontuskert Priory which is lost and covert way down in' the fields, surrounded by whitened stone walls which, from a distance, look like pearl seeds. A lark ascended slant-wise against this vista. During land drainage in the 1940s a path was discovered, a monks' pass, running from Clontuskert Priory to the ruins of a medieval church nearer to Ballinasloe – Teampoillín – which has the dramatic corbel stones typical of east Galway, the grounds of the church, verging on the Suck, having become a burial place for miscarried infants in the seventeenth century. Clontuskert Priory was rendered defunct at the end of the sixteenth century but it was ostentatiously revived in the 1630s, a brief era when beautiful chalices were made there, when, according to Protestant prelates on ecclesiastical reconnaissance and with a view to rededicating it as Protestant property, Protestants were 'unmercifully whipped and abused' in full view of the idols of the Virgin Mary.

Cromwell's men finally wrecked it. St Michael, St John the Evangelist, St Catherine of Alexandria, St Augustine stand over a doorway, accosted by a tearaway bush of furze, but otherwise it is a strange, dislocated presence against the quiet lands of the O'Kellys who planted members of their family as prebendaries and abbots there for three centuries.

Clonfert Cathedral, nine miles on, towards Offaly, was built on the site of a monastery founded by Brendan the Voyager. The saints over the Romanesque doorway have untoward grass growing in their private parts. Around it Catholic and Protestant graves have merged over the centuries but the Cathedral has been Protestant since the seventeenth century. It has always been closed when I've been there but you can peer in from one side and see the aristocratic azure of a stained-glass window.

A little boy played hurling by himself by the giant headstone of the Dowager Lady Dunboyne. A mourning family stood over a grave, boys in pastel shirts, a father. But the ancient statue of the Virgin Mary I'd seen on the ground in a corner of the graveyard last time I'd been here was missing, henna hair on her, white and gold robes, pronged crown, a Raphael-demure expression on her downcast face.

Up the road in the modern Catholic church in this land of shifting impressions of Mary is a wooden medieval statue of Madonna and child which, folklore has it, after the ravages of the seventeenth century was found up a tree, looking to its old home in Clonfert Cathedral. Mother and child have an arm missing but the child manages to hold a tress of his mother's hair, her cheeks salmon-coloured, her robes brick-coloured and chalky blue against an encasement of little festoons. This is Our Lady of Ballinasloe, Our Lady of the country and western dance-halls and the scattered churches where novenas are enunciated by old ladies on November evenings. A boy with a Mikado orange glow of dyed hair, in Dutch trousers, tended sheep on a hillock just as I crossed the Shannon at Banagher. Teenage supporters of a boxing team, in army jackets, marched through town, ignoring the strangeness of the small Victorian billiard hall with pitched roof.

It was dark by the time I reached the ruins of the medieval monastic city of Clonmacnoise, old women in black straggling among the modern graves, the ancient crosses blasted by lichen, the round towers, the neat modern paths, the discreetly side-lined yew trees – the crucified Christs with owlish faces and plasticine arms almost lost in the dark.

When I was a child we were told the tale in Ballinasloe National School, under the buxom, Victorian Protestant church, of the builder who demanded more money for finishing off the round towers, thereby irritating a bishop who pulled away the ladder when the builder was beavering away with some touch on top of a tower, at which point he, the builder, began systematically taking the tower apart. 'Sure isn't it easier to take down two stones than put up one' was the punch-line in the story and our minds imagined a bygone Clonmacnoise, turf boats with red tanned sails on the Shannon beside it. Life seems to have borne out this punch-line, as the history of Ballinasloe's monastic ruins and fretted statues had done anyway.

Later that night there was music in a roadside pub over the border in Roscommon, the lights of Athlone, the Las Vegas bravura of some of them, not far away. I'd passed a pub in Ferbane, County Offaly, which had a placard in the window saying: 'The world and his wife drinks Guinness', the wife in this advertisement, under the Arc de Triomphe revelling by a Guinness-laden table with her husband, having an early 1960s bouffant hair-do. But the pub had been closed. Maybe, with its downfall of thatch, it had been closed since the early 1960s. A three-man showband played on a small stage in the rural pub near Athlone – a scattering of photographs on a wall in an inner sanctum enmeshing a night of particular celebration in the pub – women and men in paper hats, faces ballooned by over-proximity to the camera.

> Catch me if you can
> I'm your man
> My name is Dan.

These are some of the words I picked up in the midst of a thumping guitar and a harmonica which followed it with whining but jubilant staccatos. Another song was: 'Where the strawberry beds sweep down to the Liffey'.

A man with a plenitude of black forelocks, his French-flag-red tie askew, got up from the audience to sing a song about a man who married a woman of questionable age only to find she wore a wig when he got into bed with her. The advice of the song was to wed 'a blooming nineteen-year-old damsel'. The man made an embarrassed and awkward but smiling excuse for the song before he faded from the stage, mumbling that it was for 'his other half'. An old man leaned over and told me there were ninety-one bachelors in the parish and he was the ninety-first.

Most of the people in the pub were old. The young were gone to San Francisco, Chicago. But they still got up to dance, the old, women with novelty perms, silver high heels, men with violet sheens on their cheeks. It could have been the 1950s for a moment and despite the ghostly sense of diaspora there was serene enjoyment on the women's faces, smiles which triggered off the imagination and followed you, with your headlight, through lonely bogland to the town of Ballinasloe.

Stone patterns of arched medieval windows against the sky, outlines of monasteries under pale lilac skies, the threat of suburbia, the watercolour of a buttercup running into the words of a song in a country and western stop-over pub – these were the import of this landscape.

In Ballinasloe, late at night, two convoy people, a girl and a boy, perhaps left over from the fair, walked along with a dog on a leash, the girl's hair crimson lake, a narrative pattern on her high woollen stockings, the boy's laces undone and a jumble of what looked like Christmas decorations around the dog's neck.

1991

Berlin diary

'What country, friend, is this?'

7 January 1991. I arrive in Kreuzberg on the seventh anniversary of the suicide of the young mother of a German friend. There's a lighted menorah in a window on the street. From the fourth-floor window of a house a girl is throwing bits of a Christmas tree down to a boy. A boy and a girl on opposite sides of a side street mime endearments to one another as they part. A cinnamon-coloured sausage in the window of a Turkish fast-food place is a horseshoe shape over oily stuffed vines. *My Sexcess* is showing at a corner cinema. Near the entrance to my house is a picture showing a bee entering a rhinoceros's open mouth, amid an aureole of many-coloured flowerheads.

The street is one of high, noble houses, late-nineteenth-century houses, where the middle classes lived at the front and the working classes at the back. My front room faces the street, which is dark creamy colour, where, among the lime trees, there is a blankness now and a memorial silence.

Next morning a sanguine-coloured church is nimbused distantly. The sky is butterscotch and almost spring-like and what looks like a wine-coloured wartime dress is strung on a hanger by a window of a chipping, a disintegrating façaded, glassy-green house.

12 January 1991. I take the train to Friedrichstrasse and cross what was once the border within the station.

A blond boy in motorbike boots has been eyeing his neighbour's motorbike magazine and a conversation about motorbikes starts up before we reach Friedrichstrasse. A woman beside me, who thinks I'm American, tells me of her sister who married an American army officer, lived first in Norfolk, Virginia, then moved to Missouri. 'She never had children. All she had was bulls.'

In one of the tunnels under Friedrichstrasse a man, slightly bowed, is selling catkins, holding them out in his hand.

First time I came here, in the summer of 1986, women were waiting with marguerites on the other side. It was a summer when the lucid light of Central Europe turned the zinnias being sold at corner shops along boulevards to brilliant peach, when London had seemed particularly grey and after London the light, the sunshine here was beatific, was open arms for me. There was a host of bituminous-shirted punks moving along under the faded carnelian of Liebfrauen Cathedral on my first journey into East Berlin, springing on one another's shoulders; drunken soldiery – some in clasping, tottering pairs – in Marx-Engels Park; although it was a sunny day a lady in a long pink mackintosh on Alexanderplatz, pink ice cream dribbling, seared down her face; clusters of country people, the men in check shirts, near the satellite clock on Alexanderplatz which tells the time in Phjong-jung and Guatemala City; a tattoo on the wrist of a gypsy woman with long black hair and a white braid at the back of her head.

Young girls wrapped femmer (fragile – I think I got the word in Yorkshire a year before) art postcards in salmon-coloured paper in shops by the Wall and back on the West side the Wall told me: 'Never forget the power on the right side fights with the power on the left side. We got to Berlin together. Forget East and West.'

A young man dragged a little boy by on a sleigh as I stood in front of this piece of graffiti, the sun going down over a nearby cobbled square surrounded by modern apartment blocks.

February of last year I returned to the border. A man in the costume of a carpenters' guild, in a scarlet baker's hat, stood motionlessly on the West side near an opening in the Wall, a hammer pin on his lapel. He was sixty miles from home, he said. Behind him there were lizard-skin patterns on the wall.

Young people in the voluminous apartment rooms of Kreuzberg complained. They felt cheated, disgruntled. West Berlin
drug addicts, squatters, had been excluded from the soup
kitchens in November and this contumely was still cogitated by
those many shades removed from them socially. Sculpted-
featured young people stood in pairs in the rooms of Kreuzberg,
surveying distant cups and saucers as if they were a phalanx
which was threatening them. These rooms seemed jeopardized,
these rooms which accommodated themselves to many
purposes: sleeping, cooking, eating, partying, gatherings over a
litter of philosophy books.

Back in Berlin in the month of January 1991 the atmosphere is
initially calmer, more loving, like the first time I came. The moon
in all its stages in earrings, cairns of silver studs on boots,
loganberry jackets like bits of Otto Dix brocade. A man in a
hound's-tooth hat comes up and makes a funny face at me over a
lemon cravat on the metro.

A boy from East Berlin holds out a Bavarian mug beside a
sleeping elk near Gedächtniskirche and a man uses a Lippizaner
pony to obtain money. The woman who showed little placards
saying, 'The orgasm of the Goddess is peace', 'Pity the sexual
desperation of women over thirty' near Gedächtniskirche, in
February of last year, is still here. She wears a coif now. A one-
legged man in a suit with a white hankie in his breast pocket
comes up and presses a sweet into her hand.

Walter Benjamin's punctured features are everywhere on a
poster, he who said that if the collector loses his collection he is
invalided. The Gestapo confiscated his library in Paris and he
killed himself in the Pyrenees. Berlin is like a collection of cities; it
brings a collection of cities together. Especially now with olive-
faced Romanian women in scarves of midnight blue who beg
near the Gedächtniskirche.

'I've come to Berlin to have the shit fucked out of me,' a boy
from the English Midlands tells me. He comes from a town
where the tramps take anabolic steroids and become huge-
shouldered, drink cider vinegar and eat molasses. I remember a
Jewish girl in London describing the trauma her mother under-

went first time back in Germany since the war, driving through on the way back from a holiday in Yugoslavia.

My own first journey outside Ireland keeps coming back these weeks of January, something I haven't thought about for a long time: 1968, just after the revolution, Paris, incarceration with a French family who had a reproduction of van Eyck's *Marriage of Giovanni Arnolfini* over the mantelpiece in a suburb of Paris where the apartment buildings are prune-coloured – a redundant, cap-topped, trunk-shaped building near by – and where a marma-lade-haired, demented Irish woman exile from the 1930s wan-dered through the arcade.

15 January 1991. Young people, some with hair the green of unripe bananas, bang on Coca Cola tins, on bits of corrugated iron, litter bins, biscuit tins, blow whistles, clink bicycle bells outside the Gedächtniskirche. Boys and girls, one with honey-coloured rat-tails, strum guitars and sing '*Sag mir wo die blumen sind?*' 'Where have all the flowers gone?' on the steps. Last time I heard that song was in Prague the night before the Pope came.

Narcissi and little American flags and pictures of Jan Palach and President Masaryk in a trilby everywhere.

'*Kam šly ušechry kvétiny?*'

Nuns militaristically waving little French tricolours, singing 'Alleluia', leading cohorts of young people in storming motion across bridges where boys were dressed as the Beatles under soot-black statues of St Christopher and St Marguerite, bridges blasted by crimson sun.

The sun in January in Berlin is hesitant, still spring-like.

The green and yellow sluices in the hair are a shared feature at the triangle of wasteland for the homeless at Linné in Kreuzberg. Once this triangle was a part of the East that lay on the Western side of the Wall. Now it's a caravan site, the blinking post office tower not too far behind it, terracotta funnels, high-rise apart-ment blocks wedging in the triangle.

Smoke comes out of caravans painted with red and white stripes and shaped like Yorkshire caravans, ledge-topped. Alsa-tians bound around and there's the face of a jackal on one flag and a scrabble of ultramarine on another. There are five such sites in Berlin, few squats now. A squat recently opened in East Berlin was closed by the police after eighteen hours.

It is 17 January. The war has broken out. I give money to one boy who is part of a group of figures swathed by the smoke of a fire and he follows me to return a coin from the DDR which was among the collection. Beside us, *'Pour la vie. Encore. Encore. Encore. Encore'* and *'Hurt la loi'* are scribbled on the door of a Turkish supermarket.

On 19 January at the fleamarket off Ufer Hallesches men in koofis cloak their goods on long tables in the waste ground and bicycles with trailers behind them veer towards the entrance. It began, this market, when Poles came and sold cigarettes and alcohol to Turks. Then it was closed down and fenced off. A year ago it was opened as a controlled fleamarket. The aquarelle canal surface near by, the mustard-coloured winter willows, the stretches of mud all are part of a landscape which anyone who's been to Berlin in winter recognizes as a dream part of this city, but now the dream is tinged with nightmare again.

In the evening Bach's Cantata Number 81 is sung in the Gedächtniskirche, among the little azure slabs of windows. A woman offered me Eucharist in this church during the week and I welcomed the sacrament.

> *Auch in abnehmender Frist, auch in den Wochen der Wendung.*
> *Niemand verhulfe uns jewieder zum Vollsein,*
> *Als der einsame wigene Gang uber der schaflosen Landschaft.*

Not in a waning phase, nor yet in the weeks of versation
Would there be ever one to help us to fullness again,
Save for own lone walk over the sleepless land.[1]

19 January. *Die Turtles* plays near the Gedächtniskirche. A woman and a little girl stand, both with candles, near a pool of wax which has exploded into a bonfire.

[1] Rainer Maria Rilke, 'Elegy for Marina'.

On my return from my first journey away from Ireland, at Dublin Airport, there were photographs of tanks in Prague, bicycles amid smoke. The bikes pull up and the cyclists watch now. A woman in a fur coat, a viridian ribbon through her auburn, sock-style-edged hair, carries a candle, weltered in her hands. All around are little bonfires of wax and the word *Krieg* a motif among them.

'What part of the USA are you from?' a boy with spindly lemon hair asks.

At the mention of the USA another boy tells me to forget about oil, go looking for brains.

I feel like saying 'Hell, I'm an Alabama boy', like the cups on sale in Greyhound bus stations on the borders of Alabama.

When he finds out I'm from Ireland he is brotherly. He went to school for a while in Cork. People thought him odd because he liked to walk the fields. It was considered all right to lean on a spade and stare at the landscape all day. But all the same, and paradoxically, Irish people have a powerful empathy with their own landscape which is enviable to a young German.

He is from Oldenburg in the north of Germany. There are three hundred soldiers from his town stationed in the east of Turkey near the Iraqi border.

A dumb Turkish couple make signs to one another, she with a copper beehive, he with magenta-tipped tan shoes. They sit on the steps and snoggle. 'Don't war. Take Gysi' a placard behind them says.

I walk home, through back streets, by lime trees, by churches lit up on top by red lights. The monochrome sleepless land in my mind is part Ireland, part Berlin, part the suburbs of Paris, part the suburbs of Prague.

In my apartment the catkins from Friedrichstrasse are still fresh and so are the memories of my first visit to Berlin, a journey away from wasteland after all, from back streets in Lewisham where the graffiti said 'Lady Luck and Dexter Sapphire', beside tinker encampments where vardos, stationed there in winter, emblazoned at the front with clumps of grapes, were now gone on reconnaissance.

Louise Erdrich and Michael Dorris

Whatever may befall thee, it was preordained for thee from
everlasting. Whatever happens at all happens as it should.

Marcus Aurelius

'Princess Diana, she was my rival for the affection of your prince.
We were at a dock. Charles had shown a very pointed interest in
me. And Princess Diana was driving by in a speed-boat with one
of those jaunty hats she wears with a little feather coming up.
Charles kind of saluted her but didn't really want to notice that
he and I were becoming very attached. He was looking at my
childhood scrapbook, my photographs and things like that. And
she was very, very jealous and angry.'

The dreams come when she's not writing, especially when
she's pregnant. She's playing 'First time ever I saw your face' on
the piano and Elvis Presley arrives to hear her. She doesn't
dream when she's writing but the books are dreams.

A shopkeeper's daughter is kidnapped on her wedding night,
thrown out of a car and walks, her wedding dress turned inside
out over her head 'like an umbrella', into a small Indian bar. 'Two
bare spike-heeled legs scissored with the ball, slashing lethal
arcs.'

A woman visits a dying nun whose hair is like 'a floss of
dandelions' and tries to grab a ladle from her that the nun once
used to pour boiling water into her ears.

A boy, taking the easy way, rather than feed his grandfather,
who's been hollering like Tarzan at God, the traditional remedy
for such ailments, bits of Canadian geese, gives him frozen
turkey hearts and kills him.

157

A little girl dressed as St Joseph has a fit and hits the donkey with a mallet during the convent Christmas play.

A man sits in his car on a railway track, waiting to be hit by the next train.

A young Vietnam victim is mourned by a dance, the American flag in the belt of one of the dancers, his coffin covered by a tablecloth edged with blue windmills.

A girl waits by the radio New Year 1960 for the end of the world as promised by Our Lady of Fatima and hears only the Guy Lombardo orchestra.

Princess Di's rival turns into the shadows of a small hotel room. She wears a dun trouser-suit and she is indeed beautiful, kaolin-faced, dark-haired. It is February 1988 and the hotel is not far from the Convent of the Benedictine Adorers of the Sacred Heart of Monmartre.

'One of the reasons we get along so well is that we had very similar childhoods, very similiar adolescences. Everything seemed to have a bearing on the other, our lives were so alike. We both felt isolated in our families, in our towns and in our lives. Probably that sense is part of our books.'

Their voices so overlap in talking that afterwards, unless very directly personal, you can't remember who said what, what person made which particular point and the effect in memory is like Louise Erdrich's incandescent books where characters and epochs overlay one another like trails of clouds in Midwestern winter sunsets. Michael Dorris is direct, almost teacherly in manner, though in the best sense, helping you forward when you flounder a little, his face still having a very boyish outline. Louise Erdrich's voice is quiet, mysterious, you feel she has suffered.

Talking to them in the room I sometimes imagined I was in their isolated New England farmhouse where they live with their six children, three of whom Michael Dorris adopted as a single parent when he was a very young man, he having been the first single adoptive male parent in the United States.

'Some people fall right through the hole in their lives,' one of

Louise Erdrich's characters says and I feel like that this February. It seems odd that I've met these people just now.

'Society is like this card game here, cousin. We got dealt our hand before we were even born, and as we grow, we have to play as best we can,' we are told on a highway, the Canadian border coming up.

'It's a fatalism people carry around with them. It's holding up standards against the odds. You wind up, it's the very small details that become extremely important because these are the things that are under your control,' the writers explain. Louise Erdrich was last in London when she studied here – at University College. 'We do have our colonial aspects.'

They got married just after the marriage of Prince Charles and Princess Di. To celebrate the royal wedding in Fargo where they lived there was a party on a double-decker bus at which Louise Erdrich was dressed in sandpaper and all the literati in Fargo went around to everything that was British, like Camelot Dry Cleaner's, the Empire Bar, the Tunbridge Arms which was a bunch of condominiums.

She grew up in Wahpeton, North Dakota, a small town on the Minnesota–North Dakota border, partly German, partly French, partly Chippewa, both her parents working in the Bureau of Indian Affairs boarding school. He grew up in Kentucky, part Irish, his maternal ancestors being Mannions and McGarrys from the Mayo side of County Roscommon. His family were of 'the novena-a-day, scapular medal and everything else branch of Catholicism'.

'Where I grew up, on the Feast of the Immaculate Conception at the racetrack they would have a living rosary where the horses run and it was a real honour to be a bead in the living rosary, and especially if you were an Our Father or a Mystery or a Glory Be.'

In the novel published under his name, *A Yellow Raft in Blue Water*, people are forever fleeing families. A mother tells her departing daughter not to mix with 'private eyes and gangsters'. Seattle, with its avenues of 'Chinese restaurants and Korean markets', is an escape from a Montana reservation. A woman fleeing her daughter and mother jumps into a car which turns out to be driven by her cousin. A family hand-clasp is an 'animal-trap'.

'We talk about something before writing it, show it after having written it. I tend to show Louise smaller chunks and she shows me slightly larger chunks and the other person goes over it and says this works, this needs expansion, this is not clear, this is dead in the water. And so forth. And it goes back and forth and back and forth to the point where, before we send it out, we read it aloud to each other and agree on every word.'

A Yellow Raft in Blue Water is the story of three women – daughter, mother, grandmother – as told, in turn, by themselves. *A Yellow Raft in Blue Water* is calmer than the books published under Louise Erdrich's name, except perhaps *Tracks*; it is a Flemish triptych.

'I went so many years without being a writer of fiction,' Michael Dorris says. 'I was a teacher. I write academic books. I hate my handwriting. If I can put my writing in front of me on a word-processor it looks pretty and it's more encouraging.'

Louise Erdrich had until recently always written, in contrast, in long-hand.

'Recently I've come closer to working with a word-processor. I put all the things I've written in long-hand on the word-processor, print them out, make notes in long-hand and transfer them back on. I always tend to think writing habits are just habits. Thomas Wolfe wrote on top of the refrigerator, because he was so tall.'

I'd visited Thomas Wolfe's house two months earlier where, it being the Christmas party, a woman was playing 'The Mountains of Mourne' on the piano. It was during this American trip, riding around America on Greyhound buses, that I'd started reading Louise Erdrich's books and the images I was surrounded with were like images in the books.

A heavy woman straddling on crutches was put on the bus in Knoxville, Tennessee, by a son and a husband. There had been two huge suitcases alongside her outside and she was travelling all the way to her native Iowa City for hospital treatment. 'You speak American real good,' she told me. During a thirty-six-hour stop-over at Chicago because of a snowstorm she collapsed and was taken away.

We are stranded in another snowstorm at Rollins, Wyoming, rescued by the American Red Cross, fat women in moon-boots, and put up in the McKinley Memorial Center for the night. I slept on the floor and was woken at dawn by an American ragamuffin.

On Christmas Eve a Cuban man showed me family photographs. From the East Coast he was emigrating with his children who wore almond-coloured coats, whose black hair was lustrous, the girls with magnificent red ribbons, to Sacramento, California. There was no mother in any of the photographs.

A plump girl just stared silently ahead. An orphan since birth she'd come from New York hoping to get a waitressing job in San Francisco.

One of the Greyhound stations I was stranded in, Cheyenne – eating pancakes with blueberry sauce – is one of the stop-overs in *A Yellow Raft in Blue Water*. Michael Dorris loved Greyhound buses too. He'd made a long Greyhound bus journey a few years before with three of his children after a visit to New Zealand.

'In New Zealand, people, I found when we stood in the supermarkets to check out, never spoke to one another and in the States are always chatting. I decided to get on the bus when I got back and go all the way back to New England, which is a ridiculously long time. From Los Angeles to New England in January with fourteen suitcases and three children.'

One of his adoptive children is somewhat retarded, the effects of alcohol the boy's Indian mother drank when he was in the womb, and since our meeting he's published a book about this child, *The Broken Cord*.

'I magnify and sustain those looks of understanding or compassion or curiosity that fleet across his face, fast as the breeze, unexpected at the voice of God . . .'

Perhaps it was the darkness in the room, the bleakness even, but we began talking about Catholicism.

'It's an inevitable part of the books. We think of ourselves – it keeps changing – we keep thinking of our estrangement. It becomes a metaphor for so much that happens in the lives of our characters. It's undeniably part of our lives.'

For Michael Dorris growing up 'it was complicated by all the martyrs that were killed by Indians and to be told how Isaac Jones's heart was ripped from his body and consumed by an Iroquois who was there and then a nun looking at the class. What did she think was going to happen next? But it was a surviving kind of thing. To be a Catholic was to be a minority, an embattled, surviving attitude that was tough. It had its bizarre aspects. But there was pride in that.'

For Louise Erdrich people who in 'an undramatic way are terribly faithful in their love for others' very often turn out to be Catholic.

I was going through a very bad time and they were kind. I typed up an interview afterwards. It wasn't very good. But then again there's charity in Indian philosophy as well as Catholic. The Zunis, Cochitis, Navahos have a theory that humans can't make perfect objects, to try for absolute perfection is an affront to the gods so they always make sure they have an imperfection in any work of art; weaving, pottery.

Before I left them, this couple who seemed almost, in Katherine Mansfield's phrase, to have effaced themselves so others could live through them 'in beauty and truth', Louise Erdrich and Michael Dorris gave me a piece of Indian weaving.

On the street I was met by a mad-looking boy, a kerchief around his neck, who could have been one of their characters. He had rank but lovely green eyes and I thought of a passage in *Love-Medicine* where Lipsha Morissey, part Indian, part Irish, loses himself among the dandelions, and I entered that gilded landscape, that surrogate dream, and felt, protean within myself, Indian alcoholics, suicide cases and gawkish men who wandered around Ballinasloe mental hospital when I was a child, just over the border in Roscommon, hats pulled down on their heads like punctured footballs.

Outside, the sun was hot and heavy as a hand on my back. I felt it flow down my arms, out my fingers, arrowing through the ends of the fork into the earth. With every root I prized there was return, as if I was kin to its secret lesson. The touch got stronger as I worked through the grassy afternoon. Uncurling from me like a seed out of the blackness where I was lost, the touch spread. The spiked leaves full of bitter mother's milk. A buried root. A nuisance people dig up and throw in the sun to wither. A globe of frail seeds that's indestructible.

Return to Leningrad:
a record for March 1991

This time the journey to Leningrad began in East Berlin, in the plywood interior of the S-bahn. At night East Berlin is a city of water and eyes: lighted high-rise buildings over canals.

At Lichtenberg Station a fat young man in a fur cap who had a round, baby face like Fatty Arbuckle's, an orange-buff shirt on him, loaded televisions on to the Leningrad train. In the buffet there was an ancient advertisement for Coca Cola, a woman with side-swept hair in a cranberry-coloured dress.

A little coal stove flamed at the entrance to each carriage to heat the samovar, a birch-twig broom beneath it. The woman making tea in my carriage had fading yellow mimosa in her compartment.

Poland is an hour away. The fields were sliced by trails of snow. In almost each field was a warranty of God or Mary; a crucifix in a pen, a Turkish-blue Marian grotto. Children, bearing satchels on their backs, walked very erectly to school. When I was a child at school we were told how Maud Gonne got the train to Russia, a revolver and espionage plans under her dress. She was met at the Russian border by a wood-burning train.

For me and the Lithuanians who were my companions for the present the first sight of Russia was Belorussia, ice melting on the river Memel, the onion domes of a church above it, a pheasant hopping between pine trees, a graveyard dotted with iron crosses which had three pairs of arms.

There is half a mile between Warsaw Station in Leningrad and Baltic Metro and a little man carries your baggage on a hand-drawn wagon, a procession behind him. A woman at the front of the crowd, on this occasion, carried a Lithuanian Easter banner which gave the crowd more of a processional feeling, herbs and flowers dyed alizarin and fluorescent green on the banner.

Brides with pearl-seeds on their dresses still danced at the Metropole Restaurant to Buddy Holly's 'Peggy Sue', their mothers wrapped in shawls of green and raging fuchsine. Students still dined at the Kazan Café with its translucent festoons and its adornments of giant paper hollyhocks. Karate and Hare Krishna magazines caused a sensation on Nevsky Prospect, drawing crowds around tables. But a woman in a dress patterned with red bellflowers cried in front of tall amber candles in the church at Kuznechnyy Lane. A hairdresser, herself with mussed black hair, her eye shadow cerulean and her lipstick peach, looked sadly out at the black horses against the water of the Fontanka Canal and the dark honey-coloured houses by the canal. My guides had gone, street traders I'd met my first time in Leningrad, December 1988. They were working in a deluxe dinner place in New York, serving coffee in polystyrene cups over laminated tables.

My second and most recent visit to Leningrad had been in June 1989, when women had frequently confronted me on the street asking the way to the nearest lottery booth; and in a shooting gallery women and youths had taken shots at an elephant in a Chevy convertible. I'd met the street traders by arrangement, Midsummer's evening, on the Neva embankment under the Palace of Youth. They'd flagged down an empty bus and asked the driver to drive us to a late-evening off-licence. On the way the driver stopped and picked up two American teachers, a man and woman from somewhere like Strongsville, Ohio. The off-licence turned out to be a youth sitting philosophically on a bench in a little park, bottles of wine and champagne under the bench.

We sailed up the Neva that night, getting a lecture on Leningrad from a body builder, such sights as the KGB head-quarters, down the river from the Winter Palace, lit up in rose, pointed out to us.

'His hair was yellow, and his eyes were pale blue,' the poet Esenin said of himself, and Ainis, the street trader who invited me to dinner the following night, had hair the pale of an arctic waste and cobalt eyes. Another body builder came with us. A line of women, many in poppy-red scarves, sitting in evening penumbra, howled with laughter at me in my shorts as I passed them. Ainis's landlady had an Estonian nude pin-up on the wall. She'd paid a week's wages for it. The body builder was meeting the landlady for the first time but nevertheless, before dessert, they disappeared and emerged fifteen minutes later in baby-doll dressing-gowns. I could see why Ainis and his friends fled Leningrad.

This time people lined for bread and milk outside fortification-like supermarkets in the suburbs. A young person brought me to a rock club on Kalyayeva Street which had just been burnt down by the Russian mafia. A row of penal-looking young people sat among the ruins, their heads achingly and not quite correctly bald, strumming guitars, singing a song about a hungry fiend, the words 'You'll be forever young' on the wall, a chalk portrait of Victor Soi, the Russian pop star martyred by the Russian mafia.

In courtyards of high-rise estates people stood around with strange, ragged, overgrown dogs on leashes. I'd visited some of the communal flats of Leningrad, a laundry at the front, a kitchen at the back, rooms off the corridor between jammed more with talismans than with necessities. But at the Jazz Club of Leningrad I met some young people who were staying in Leningrad and wanted to stay for ever.

Around us were women in décolleté dresses and men in John Lurie type attire, loose-fitting suits, pattern-spangled ties. A woman with a Minnie Mouse hair-do, in a black over-the-knees dress, sang a Louis Armstrong number.

> My only sin is the colour of my skin.
> What did I do to be so black and blue?

Valentina was the only one who spoke English. She was a history student. She had night-black hair, lipstick the orange of a Californian poppy, skin the pale Nadia Mandelstam, the chronicler of Russia in the twentieth century, says comes from washing in the waters of the Neva. Valentina wore a bit of black foulard around her neck. Other girls in the group wore bits of leopard-skin-pattern foulard. One of the boys had a fountain of curls, his jersey cerise, his trousers striped bags. Another wore a T-shirt with the words 'Who dun it?' on it. They were all students, either of history or economics.

To the sound of a Ray Noble number in the background Valentina began reciting a poem by Osip Mandelstam on a couch in the foyer.

> I returned to my city, familiar as tears,
> As veins, as mumps from childhood years.

They invited me with them that night and I went to the flat of a boy, on Ligovsky Prospect, whose parents were away. His father, a naval officer, was at sea and his mother was visiting Sweden. Ordinarily he slept in the same bedroom with them. The walls on the staircase had been painted cream and pale cobalt.

There was a miaowing ceramic cat on the mantelpiece and two frolicking fish, and not far from the mantelpiece a cabinet bedecked with poppies and yellow tulips. The drawing room for all its smallness was bedecked with pictures. A large picture of laminated poppies in a gilt frame. A wedding photograph of the boy's parents, a red sash around the bridal gown. A honeymoon photograph at Alpatha on the Black Sea, a monkey in an A-line dress sitting on his mother's shoulder, the monkey's hair in corn braids. There were many tiny pictures in frames; hares dancing with dachshunds, one of a cottage, milkweed and giant sun-flowers outside it. On the floor was an Armenian carpet pat-terned with nightingales.

It was the writer Liam O'Flaherty who said that Leningrad could never be taken as a tourist city: one had to go back again and again to get acquainted with it, to understand it. On that Armenian carpet I thought of his words and I thought of the poet Esenin, the 'tender hooligan' of Leningrad, imagining his face against the runny gold ikons of St Isaac's. It was as if a face, not a city, were becoming clearer to me.

We were served Moldavian cognac, pear juice, and then tea – the tea bags direct from Sri Lanka – in red dappled cups. Peanuts in a glass and a saucer of golden raisins were placed on a little table.

A boy in a peach jacket showed us photographs of a holiday he'd recently spent with a black family in New York. In one he wore a Santa Claus hat in Jefferson's home against the emerald of Maryland. He'd met a boy from this family, French-speaking like himself, on Nevsky Prospect, and subsequently got an invitation. All over the Kürfurstendamm in Berlin before I'd left had been newspapers with blobbed photographs of mass demonstrations in Russian cities. Could it be that the freedom of voyages like this boy's would soon be over?

Valentina said she loved Leningrad more than anything for its writers. Especially Anna Akhmatova.

I'd first picked up poetry by Anna Akhmatova in translation by Richard McKane on a bookstall by the river Liffey in the early 1970s.

In 1977 on a Greek island I met an Irish poet who'd spoken to her in a Dominican convent garden in Sicily in 1964 when she got the Taormina Prize.

In 1987, near a launching pad in Florida, I found I was talking to the translator of her complete works.

At Ainis's dinner party in 1989 I'd noticed her picture on the calendar. The following day was her centenary and I went to Komarova, where she lived in her later years and where she's buried.

The day after the party in Ligovsky Prospect I went back to Komarova which is about an hour north of Leningrad. On the train from Finland Station a bulldog kept nuzzling his master, a boy in a fur hat. People on skis propelled themselves with sticks on the Lake of Pikes. Snow tumbled against the sunlight from the branches of pines and the sun was bolled into the upper shadows of the pines. Akhmatova's little house was luminous turquoise in the snow.

She was the poet of Leningrad who lost two husbands, one executed, one to the camps, her son twice incarcerated for long periods because he was her son. For thirty years she could not write down her poetry and brought friends into the street to recite it, making sure they remembered it correctly.

Now she seems not just the poet of the prison queues but the poet of the romantic lonely in any system. 'Somewhere in the dull suburbs there is a lonely house.' The woman who at the time of the mass purges would come to dinner in a black silk dressing-gown, a little torn, with white dragons embroidered on it; the woman who always knelt before the ikon of the Virgin Mary before going out.

The following day I visited the room she lived in in Fontanka House, between the Fontanka Canal and Liteynyy Prospect, before she moved to Komarova. There were labyrinths of courtyards, the houses painted yellow, tall limes growing in the courtyards. The hooded lightshade is skew-ways in her room. There is a photograph of her, grief charcoaled into her face, a sketch of her in a summer dress in Tashkent during the war. It was in this room she met Isaiah Berlin in 1945.

> We met in an unbelievable year,
> When the world's strength had already been drained.

He was the second foreigner she'd encountered since the Revolution.

In a bookstore on Nevsky Prospect a salesgirl had pressed an ancient book of Leningrad photographs into my hand. It was selling for fifty roubles. She was delighted when I purchased it, a samizdat exchange between our eyes. She knew I'd give it as a gift to a person who deserved it.

In the Writers' Bookstore on Nevsky Prospect in November 1945 Isaiah Berlin, a British delegate in Moscow then, had spoken to a critic who asked him if he'd like to meet Anna Akhmatova. She had not been heard of since before the Revolution and, for him, it was like being asked if he wished to meet Christina Rossetti. He was led to Anna Akhmatova's room but the encounter was disrupted by Randolph Churchill screaming from the courtyard. He wanted help to refrigerate some caviare. Isaiah

Berlin returned that evening, spent a night in conversation with Anna Akhmatova, and met her again in January 1946 before he returned to England. Years later, on the occasion of her honorary degree at Oxford, she told him she'd felt their encounters had started the Cold War.

In the vestibule of the National Gallery in London there is a mosaic of her by her friend Boris Anrep, entitled 'Compassion', and when I visited London briefly at Easter I noticed that, despite the fact a customs official had been unpleasant to her on her one visit to England, her ikon had seeped through, a portrait of her by Olga Lyudvigovna Della-Vos-Kardovskaya all over the London underground, a carnelian shawl on her arm.

In the evening of the day I visited Fontanka House I went to the Jazz Club again and the young people, despite the fact they said they were poor, were there again, sitting in the foyer over plates of dwarf apples and dwarf meringues, some of them sipping cognac. They'd told me they'd probably manage to get back here before I left. Around us were black and white photographs of black American women singers, their mouths welling in song. 'The best thing is understanding between two people,' I'd once heard an old black man say to himself at the back of a bus in Alabama. It was as if I'd willed these young people back.

I don't know where they got their money. I didn't ask them. I'd like to have known more about them but conversation had to be phrases, photographs.

In most places where you travel you're a camera but sometimes the camera shatters and you're moved. I was moved by their loveliness, by their theatricality, by their determination to put on a romantic show in a city where people queued half a mile for jewellery. I was moved by their eyes which seemed to stress the importance of being brave, of not being cowed by things, of trying to communicate no matter what. 'Who were we anyway?' Pasternak wrote, about people who met against shadowed times.

When I reached Nevsky Prospect after leaving them it suddenly snowed and within minutes the street was mantled in snow and everyone was oblique and people straggled across the street. I thought of Maud Gonne who'd stayed three months at the Hotel de Europe, of W. B. Yeats's great love for her and his pursuit of her. 'I will find out where she has gone.' It was as if I knew that night she and people like her had gone.

Women were waiting at Warsaw Station on Saturday night, asking people to post letters in Berlin for them. A woman embraced her son and didn't want to let go of him. The train was crowded with young Leningraders who were going to work in Leningrad's twin town, Hamburg. A woman's bag bulged open and you could see the bouquet patterns on a dress.

By Sunday evening in Poland, St Patrick's Day, the young Leningraders had their sleeves rolled up and they were singing a song about Leningrad, an old lady with a white woollen cap pulled down over her ears waving a fork-like object with little cymbals on it.

At Easter, in Berlin I got an Easter card from one of those young people who could not speak English but had managed to have the message translated: 'I am writing to you, to congratulate you with the Easter.'

Sean O'Faolain: a journey

The brain recalls just what the muscles grope for: no more, no
less; and its resultant sum is usually incorrect and false and
worthy only of the name of dream.

William Faulkner

In Paris in 1968, first time outside Ireland, I found Sean O'Faolain's *An Irish Journey* in the apartment in which I was staying.
Just inside the cover a Paul Henry illustration, a purple mountain
with a pansy sheen. Berlin 1991, among the trussed belongings
of a German student in a series of cramped rooms, I found the
same book. A gift from a farmhouse in County Cork where his
mother had helped with the harvests.

The memories it brought back: a face on a brand-new passport,
freckles like bullets, bleached white Aran sweater, a prisoner's
hair-cut. The first chestnuts in the Luxemburg Gardens.

And then the bits I recognized: Sean O'Faolain being fastened
in Castlecomer by the sound of Slievenamban from Athlone; the
trees on Mardyke Lane in Cork tarred to prevent lovers from
hiding behind them; the faces of drowned children in photographs on Cape Clear.

Paris 1968 there'd been a tiredness after the student revolution
and a lot of rain. Ice creams were lavender, dove-grey and
almond-green. Sometimes someone with a pastel face, in soot,
flared trousers, ricocheting shoulder-length hair, would look
into your face with anxiety but no briefing.

Berlin 1991 Romanian women intermittently sang ditties over
their ribbon-festooned little girls as they implored for money,

girls in trouser suits played with Hula-Hoops around their waists, the grace of old men on the streets was impeccable.

Back in London in July I thought with remorse of another Sean O'Faolain book, *Vive Moi!* England 'cold like Euston in the early morning'. Edna O'Brien gave mettlesome words to the Euston purgatory. 'Euston Station was a jungle, grim and impersonal, the very pigeons looked man-made . . . This was to be home. It had nothing to recommend it. Unhealthy, unfriendly, mortarish and to my ignorant eyes morbid.' But I was brought to Euston by something.

In 1968 Sean O'Faolain's *An Irish Journey* should have warned me of what lay ahead; Dublin, the city to fall in love in but also one that can wreak vengeance on those who don't altogether go with its agenda.

Sean O'Faolain quoted Bernard Shaw to describe what was most pernicious and yet incipient about Dublin: 'A certain flippant, futile derision and belittlement that confuses the noble and serious with the base and ludicrous seems to be peculiar to Dublin.' And he conceived it as a city of eclipsed rats: 'No sooner does any man attempt, achieve, here, anything fine than the rats begin to emerge from the sewers . . .'

But it was to Dublin Sean O'Faolain decided to return to preserve the integrity of the eighteen-year-old in him. To achieve this Edna O'Brien stayed on in the world of Euston. Another Cork man, Willy Quinton, in William Trevor's *Fools of Fortune*, went further to preserve this intactness. 'I returned to Italy, to my world of Ghirlandaio, to my Canary roses and my irises.' But some of Sean O'Faolain's characters make a necessary journey in this direction too. England is a memory to be disparaged in Paris in *Before the Daystar*, Paris, the city of triumph where, in the 1920s, the floundering old aristocrat Henn led his tinker leman who flaunted a big hat with a feather in it.

For many Irish people England, the country between Ireland and Europe, is a purgatorial world not unlike Lough Derg in *Lovers of the Lake*. 'A sensation of the world's death.' Or at least that's the way it used to be. Now, newly, it's alive and tormented and barbaric in its own way. 'We're ninety degrees. Beating Greece and Turkey.'

In the summer of 1991 the shop where I got old seaside humour cards is closed down and England doesn't seem a place to be.

In the British Library I read Sean O'Faolain's evocation of Ballinasloe, the town I was born in, 'undistinguished houses' which lay on 'a slight ridge that alone seemed to keep the whole place from sinking into the bog to its chimney tops'. His wife, Eileen, taught there in the 1920s and developed a 'growing terror' she might never escape from it and if she did she'd find herself in 'another, identical Ballinasloe'.

In the same book, *Vive Moi!*, I meet one of my own characters, Belle Bilton, the London music-hall artiste who married a local lord. Sean O'Faolain spoke to a former stable boy who remembered her driving a pair of greys along Main Street, scarlet trappings on them, she in a red coat, 'going, he said, he knew not where and it might be that she herself sometimes did not know either'. For Sean O'Faolain the October Horse Fair was the only exciting event in Ballinasloe and afterwards it would 'sink back into the silence to its bog grave for the rest of the year'.

But he did not notice one shadowy-season event in Ballinasloe: the coming of the barn-storming players. In the summer of 1991 I return to Galway, from Berlin via London, to try to find their aura, their stellar beacons on the fair-green. 'If once the boy within us ceases to speak to the man who enfolds him, the shape of life is broken and there is, literally, no more to be said. I think that if my life has had any shape it is this. I have gone on listening and remembering. It is your shape, O my youth, O my country.'

They were there in the 1920s and they came right up to the early 1960s. In Berlin when I thought of Ireland it was of them, more than anything, I thought. The bravery. The resilience.

'No I won't go in. It's not evening. It's just the afternoon,' I make Belle Bilton say on the veranda of a Georgian house in an east Galway summer, one of those summers of radiant bog-cotton and of strawberry clover.

1991

I want to find again the after-glow of a performance in a marquee on the fair-green, to return to the eighteen-year-old, to shield him now against all that is going to lash at him.

My country, a journey.

Guatemala

Cobán. 7 August 1991. The last night of the feria. Young students from the military school who have mohawk hair-cuts, the sides of whose heads are old gold, dance on a platform under a tent broadly striped like a golf umbrella as a deaf and dumb man in indigo raingear wanders around with a simpleton's smile among the Indian women who are seated with their babies on fold-up chairs slashed with violet Pepsi Cola signs, staring at the dancers who demonstrate the latest dances to Madonna numbers. The nearby carousel – griffins, basilisks, ducks – carries old Indian women with near-black, knitted and serious faces as the dancers follow mandates: 'Stick out your butt and shake what you got.'

Not too far away is a marquee, guarded by chary teenage soldiers, with an exhibition of military photographs – the military organizing a beauty competition for Indians in the Alta Verapaz Highlands. The winner of this competition, stooping, wears a white veil over her terracotta dress. A military video shows the beauty of Guatemala – white nun orchids, macaws of orange and glitter blue, frail monkeys with whisked frizzes of hair and bereaved, human-flesh faces.

Glenn, one of my travelling companions, the sides of whose face are incandesced in a young medieval saint's beard, starts talking to Whitney who works with the fair. He ran away from San José eight years ago when he was twelve and he claims his face, as that of a missing person, is on milk cartons in the United States. A child goes by with a *piñata*, one of those huge Guatemalan papier-mâché dolls, many colours in them, this one predominantly poppy and electric blue.

176

Next day Whitney stands among the gathered bits of wood from a rail track which look like shavings. The slashes all over his jeans are wigs, an albino's hair. He loves Guatemala, loves the life of the fair, but even he has seen *el panel de la muerte* – the van in which death squads took victims who were very often later found with their throats slashed to the point of decapitation or in some cases skinned. *El panel de la muerte* has frequently passed through this country since the mid 1960s, where clouds fall asunder and dig into the tops of volcanoes, where movement often seems like a trespass so still are the reflections of a slate-blue volcano on a lake, so myriad and silent and personably voluptuous are the blues of the hills.

About two hundred thousand people have been killed, under the hotchpotch rule of generals, colonels, brigadiers, since the early 1960s. Forty thousand people have disappeared since the early 1980s. When civilian rule came in 1985, especially towards the end of the term of office of President Vinicio Cerezo, hundreds continued to die. Now with the accession of President Jorge Serrano there are signs calling for peace and reconciliation everywhere, little doves on the fringes of them.

On the night before I arrived, 31 July, the body of a seven- or eight-year-old street child was found in a rubbish dump beside an electric pylon in Zona 3 of Guatemala City, his eyes gouged out. On 1 August, the day I arrived, a street child who'd pinched sunglasses in the central market was taken and tortured with cigarette butts on the testicles by the police. On 8 August Jose Miguel Merida Escobar, head of the homicide section of the Department of Investigations, was gunned down in Guatemala City. He'd been investigating the murder last year of an anthropologist who worked with Indians. The couple I stayed with in Cobán had exchanged love letters during the Highland campaign of the early 1980s. The husband had been a doctor with the army. Nothing in El Salvador, he said, could have been as bad as what he saw.

A head of Christ and some severed plaster hands of saints were affixed to a wall hanging.

When the army wiped out an Indian village during the

177

Highland campaign they usually stuck one face on a tree as the expression of mastery.

General Mejía Victores, who came to power in 1983, destroyed four hundred and forty villages, killing one hundred thousand people.

In the couple's home, beside the wall hanging, was a picture of Lassie, a crucifix with oregano, sage and thyme thrust through it, a photograph of a baptism, a picture of a muscular-faced Apollo 7 astronaut.

In Guatemala, where there is no public health programme, chopping off hands and feet is still a way of dealing with gangrene. The government of Jacobo Arbenz, who came to power in 1950, tried to bring health care to all. But President Eisenhower and the CIA and the United Fruit Company put an end to his government in 1954 with a coup that was followed by hundreds of killings.

A young man in a smouldering pink and apple-green tie had driven a Kaiser Manhattan 1954, of cream and royal blue, through the fair, a collection of girls in the car with 1950s hair-dos and wearing peplum dresses, the dresses with boleros that stick out at the waist.

In 1963 President Kennedy was responsible for bringing down another vaguely egalitarian government.

'The rivers have been running with blood since the early seventies,' my hostess in Cobán told me.

During the late 1970s, under the rule of General Lucas García, having a small group of people in your house was an invitation to *el panel de la muerte*.

My hostess knew a vendor of nick-nacks who went into the mountains in Alta Verapaz in the early 1980s and was shot by the army because he hadn't got his papers. In 1982 Ríos Montt of the Inglesia del Verbo was in control. He ardently preached evangelism during his one year of dictatorship and now in every Indian village there are up to half a dozen evangelist huts and it is not uncommon to see Indian women or poor *ladino* women stretched out, beating the ground at night, possessed by the Holy Spirit while a man plays the accordion and croons lullaby-hymns.

Inglesia Assamblea Dios Bethsaida, Inglesia Evangelica Cuadrangular, Inglesia Evangelica Bautista Gethsemani, Templo Evangelico Emmanuel, Inglesia de Dios Pentecostes, Templo Assamblea de Dios Salem, Inglesia El Redentor are reverberations of General Ríos Montt, usually poor, dusty places, often with drums and keyboards. General Ríos Montt, a man still praised because he had delinquents shot, a man whose boring sermons preached on television every Sunday night are still voodoo. 'I don't steal. I don't lie. I don't abuse,' was his pabulum for the country.

'*No mas secestros*', 'No more kidnappings', a slogan said on a wall in the red-light district of Zona I in Guatemala City.

It was raining and all that could be seen of female prostitutes were their legs sticking out from under long sheets of plastic. A male prostitute in a glitter suit played with a lighted yo-yo by the kerb.

The first breath-in of this country, under skies which could have been the cloud skies of Knock, had been the giant, cupola churches of Guatemala City which seemed to flinch – the memory of murder or earthquake? – and the Spanish colonial churches the colour of pig pigment. Inside these churches saints held up infants wrapped in chiffon as if they were about to throw them. Indian women clung to the brown garb of a saint and the Virgin was lined up like women in a beauty competition – Our Lady of San Juan, Our Lady of Guadalupe, Our Lady of Mercedes, Our Lady of Desamperados, the Immaculate Conception, Our Lady standing on a half-moon, Our Lady standing on a lamb. They had the look of 1950s Italian stars, black or hennaed hair, vaguely febrile faces.

The most popular was Our Lady of Desamperados, Our Lady of the Abandoned. Two street children prayed in front of her, one with a turtle-brown face, his white teeth gleaming as he prayed. They followed me outside afterwards. There were ancient black and white photographs stuck behind Our Lady of Desamperados, a youth, one leg astride on stone steps. Christ often lay like a caged animal in a glass cage, sometimes silvered ocelot skin on him. If he was standing the favourite colour of his garb seemed to be bluebell blue with a confetti of thorns on his head.

Men with rose-madder and cobalt typewriters had typed passport applications on the streets in Guatemala City. Jesuit magazines ranged alongside those showing near-nude and masked wrestlers or by booklets about the splendours of sex. Towels from El Salvador were exhibition pieces in shops; they showed tableaux of peace – women washing by brooks, ox-drawn ploughs in the fields, a turtle on its journey. There were painted flowers made of corn husks on the wall of a restaurant with all the signs of the zodiac on the floor. The faces in record-shop windows were mainly of Franco de Vita and Tres Voces de El Salvador.

The journey through Guatemala had been on protruding-nosed buses painted in carousel colours, past towns where Indian women vendors sprinkled yogurt with cinnamon, where candles burned at evening on sky-blue weighing scales on market stalls under runny volcanos, where Maria Montes stood in the nude in *barberíe* alongside Virgin Marys with stamens of gold on their head.

There were Chinese restaurants in every town and village, long-necked birds, swans, dragons trussed together outside them. 'Why are there so many Chinese people?' I asked my hostess in Cobán. 'Because Milton Cerezo, the brother of President Vinicio Cerezo, offered Chinese people citizenship for eight thousand dollars.' But then again she told me that the government in El Salvador pays the guerrillas so that American aid keeps coming every day. She also told me that when aid came after the 1976 earthquake the streets of Guatemala City were chock-a-block with Mercedes. That I had no trouble believing.

By Lake Atitlán there were miles of tourist stalls, huge hangings haunted by the faces of little merchants who stood in front of them. But the casualties mix with the tourists. In 1988 an epileptic boy who went looking for firewood outside San Lucas Tolimán near Lake Atitlán disappeared as did two of his relatives who went in search of him. The army was in the area at the time. Last December, in Sololá, overlooking the lake, fifteen people, including three children, were mowed down by the army when they appeared at an army base to protest against army pillaging.

In the fields on my journey had been the red blooms of coral trees, trees with huge white bells on them – the cartucho tree. There were young soldiers with M16s all over the roads as there had been security men with M16s outside every second store in Guatemala City. A bridge on the way to Cobán had just been blown up so we had to go another way. The power in Guatemala City was cut off for three days just after we'd left it, a power station blown up, and cholera was confirmed at the same time.

'I came to this hotel and went to a picture house where I met a dumb whore . . .' Urine merged with the flooding from the showers in a hotel. On my door there were weavings of graffiti. *'La muer que entre aqui acompañada es para yique?'*

I'd come here with two American students. We'd met in a bar in Alabama in December and made a pact to come here as a woman in country-and-western gear sang a Patsy Kline number – 'I cried all the way to the altar' – to fat women in male dress perched on tables. Sandra, one of my companions, led anti-war protests of five people around an orange-buff clock tower called Denny Chimes in Tuscaloosa, Alabama, in January.

Beside the billboards with peace signs were billboards with posters of nudes, a nude with Alka Seltzer scrawled across her stomach, a nude with a battery in her pubic parts; on buses people stared into a little magazine which showed preening nude women among an array of mutilated and preferably nude corpses – prostitutes found murdered in Guatemala City or San Salvador, street children murdered by the police in Guatemala City, the victims of death squads in El Salvador, guerrillas found murdered near the power station which was blown up.

In small towns lyceum boys paraded with the goose step, immaculate white bands crossed on their chests, necklaces of regalia around their necks, plumes in their caps. They paraded past graffiti of blue and red and pink. On one parade there were fire brigades, each with its *madrina*, its beauty queen.

The confessional boxes in churches looked as if they were for dolls. Beside the statues of Dominic Savio and St Beatrice de Silva

in small churches were altars for recent martyrs, priests, cat-
echists, agronomists killed in 1981, 1982, their photographs
honoured with white ribbons.

All over Guatemala *'Dos nacos en el planeta de las mujeres'* was
playing, two simpletons in G-strings confronting a synod of
Amazons. The second most popular film was *Los Mercenarios
Implacables* with Miles O'Keefe.

The stacks of postcards all over Guatemala City had prepared
me for this country, postcards showing young Indian men
dressed as centurions, wearing saffron cloaks, postcards barred
with fuchsine and indigo, the predominant colours of costume.
But there was another, never to be erased stack of postcards,
nuns in white bearing the coffin of an Indian woman who'd died
in childbirth, street children throwing paper flowers and white
crêpe over a murdered comrade, street children bearing the
coffin of a murdered comrade, street children keeping vigil
around the coffin of their comrade, street children with their ears
cut off and their eyes either burnt or gouged out, bodies being
recouped from the secret, mass graves of the early 1980s.

In El Quiché, during one such excavation, the firemen played
football with the skulls.

Poverty is the man with a missing hand; shanty towns built on
landfills; restaurants with no running water where smells are
drowned out with *pom*, a sacrificial incense; a legless boy on a
rollerboard holding up a gallows from which a row of pink
candyfloss hangs. Hope is nearly always the Virgin Mary, the
edges of her garments; a child, a child in white bobby socks and a
coral party dress with fiery edges to the frills. The bus of gentian
blue and flamingo pink, *'flor de mi tierra'*, didn't stop for an Indian
woman and her two small children but it stopped down the road
for a *ladino* woman with pastel lipstick.

In banks in little villages there were usually four queues,
traveller's cheques, savings, cashing regular cheques, payments.
The Indians were always queuing to pay.

Black people cling to the coast where the *almendra*, the almond
tree, turns carmine by the sea in late August, where little black
boys with amber and gold in their hair gesticulate their penises at

the sea, where the vultures gather like black crêpe on shores flanked by tendril-like coconut palms. 'Martin Luther King. Bob Marley. Nelson Mandela dueho,' is carved on a tree.

Raddled tennis shoes are piled up with teddybears, Alka Seltzer, aspirins, soup-mixes and bikinis in stores on the sea front.

At night, to the sound of reggae, there's a run on cornflakes which are lit up by kerosene lamps.

'*Guatemala tu nombre es immortal*,' says the carthartic sign on a beach. Miami Vice is the name of a brothel and a black boy on the brothel steps has picked up a card: 'La Cadavera'.

'*Como se llama*?' I ask a little *ladino* boy in a blouse of lacquer red on the shore at night.

'Anton.'

I start walking away and he runs after me.

In the night of chalcedony and smoke a little black boy pulls another little black boy along on a dried-milk tin.

I buy Anton pink nougat sweets from El Salvador which have candied fruit in them and my pretend parenthood is done. He hurries away.

Back at Houston Airport an American man is saying loudly into the telephone: 'I don't want to play games with you. I've seen enough games in Central America. I've no sentiment left for you and I don't want to go home.'

I've no sentiment left for you, I thought, and I don't want to go home, and like Whitney who ran away from San José I want to go on travelling to ferias where the stalls are sprinkled with the Tarot – La Rosa, La Sirena – where *mariache* bands in maroon suits and in black velvet dicky bows play *ranchera* music – three-chord progression music – where men in sombreros take aim in shooting galleries over the mass graves of pink mice.

St Petersburg at the New Year: a love story

3 January 1992. I walk arm in arm with a baby-owl of a man who carries a briefcase through the courtyard of the Academy of Arts. The clouded sky is cherry-coloured and amaranth purple with evening and the lights of the windows are golden in the rain. Ice has been melting and the cobblestones are treacherous in the rain and we pick our way in a mutal pose of supplication.

'It's raining cats and dogs. Or, as we say in Russia, the rain is coming down in buckets. *Cabaret* with Liza Minnelli is a beautiful film. What did they see wrong that we couldn't see it for years? Sex? You can't have sex without beauty. Now you can see everything. And a lot more. You know the joke? What the Russian girl says to the Englishman? There's no sex in Russia. I was born in the Ukraine. Evacuated to Tashkent. Came to live in St Petersburg after the war. My heart is not in it any more. It's too difficult. Five years ago we had fruit and vegetables and meat like the other big cities. Now the provinces keep the food for themselves.'

Just outside the courtyard, on the pavement, he lets go of my arm and tries to step on to the road. He falls into a cleft of water to his waist. 'Oh, my skeleton is pained!' he shouts. I wipe his briefcase with tissues.

We get on a bus and go to an ice-cream parlour on Nevsky Prospect where I buy him ice-cream and fruit cocktail, served by a woman in peep-toe, moccasin sandals with black net uppers. A little girl with a bouquet effect of ribbon on her head drifts around waving a carrot-haired doll and at a nearby table young soldiers, some in turquoise fur hats, some in forage caps, have half tuned into our conversation as has a girl in a leopardskin trousers at another nearby table. At the next table to us a woman is treating her children to ice-cream but despite her tasselled silk shawl her face is the face of famine.

Why do I think of Dublin in the 1950s? Going there at Christmas with my father and mother. To the races at Fairyhouse or the pantomime at the Gaiety which boasted the most ungainly sisters, Maureen Potter and a man with Nordic blond hair with braids. The ugly sisters in the Gaiety pantomime would wander around the stage like two nuns out for a walk together in Ballinasloe, huddled up and close in conversation.

> Stop and consider! Life is but a day;
> A fragile dew-drop on its perilous way
> From a tree's summit.

On those trips to Dublin with my parents as a child I saw men march, singing 'Starvation Once Again', I saw women march, holding pictures of Cardinal Mindszenty; later on I held my mother's hand as we watched Brendan Behan's funeral.

The baths at Marata Street feel like Dublin's baths in the 1950s. On 3 January naked men beat themselves with bits of Christmas tree. A tap haemorrhages on to a bowl containing a piece of Christmas tree. In the sauna a rosé man feeds water into the oven which is built into the wall and has shutters on it. At one point I come into the sauna and it is empty but for a nude pearl child crouching in red sandals among the bits of Christmas tree which are scattered everywhere. At another point I come into the sauna and it is crowded with naked men wearing woollen caps, all on their hunkers, chanting a strange song which could be a rugby song or a Christmas hymn. Outside the sauna a man is bent over as another man creams him with shampoo, and a man whose entire back is tattooed is seated talking to a friend, the tattoo depicting a Russian Orthodox priest holding up a cross against a medieval Batman-type figure with a ponderous crotch.

The walls are lemon and they are slimy the way the walls of the changing rooms in Blackrock Baths were slimy when I was a child, and I think of the outdoor Blackrock pool, just a wall keeping us from the Irish Sea and what lay beyond, the pestilence called England. The outer rim of the Blackrock pool was strong as an Iron Curtain.

One night, after a day when we swam at Blackrock Baths, my father took me to an outdoor performance of *Twelfth Night* in Blackrock Park. There were lights around the park like the lights in parts of Petersburg now, red, blue, green, white. Nevsky Prospect is ruled by different departments and only one part, near Moscow Station, has lights, white lights like a row of deep-fronted necklaces.

On New Year's Eve at Prospect Prosveshchenlya, a new town to the north, my friend Denis played 'Going home' by Rockin' Ronnie and 'Let's go to the hop' by Danny and the Juniors on a sausage-like cassette player, and drunks in fur hats came up to jive. Resigned-looking men in brackish furs stood at stalls around us, selling Sharon fruit. A woman studied two identical henna rubber dogs for a quarter of an hour before purchasing one. The doors of a truck were thrown open with a poster showing a sylvan scene – brooks, mountains under blushed skies – pinned on either side and there was a run on such posters, a man, crouched, handing them down to a queue. Fires burned in huge rubbish canisters under the star-blue high-rises and little trains of people carrying Christmas trees were charcoaled into the snow wastes in front of the flats.

Denis was wearing bi-coloured teddy-boy spats he'd bought in London, forks of white through the black on top. He'd taken a plane to London in October, lost everybody's address on the way, met his Russian friend Dimitriy in Victoria Station on the day of his arrival, shacked up with Dimitriy in a room on the King's Road for a month. Dimitriy got £30 a week, immigrant's money, from the Queen, and a free room.

In London Denis saw Marlon Brando in *The Wild One* but to him the seventeen-year-olds were more like thirty-five-year-olds. All they thought about was money. He'd corrugate his forehead and point a finger at it to show this. He returned to St Petersburg. Despite everything his friends and he had fun all the time there. Gena, one of his friends, was a bouncer in a café and I had a sauna with them at the back of the café my first night in St Petersburg this time.

Gena slept on work nights in a room near the café, his bed surrounded by weight-lifting contraptions which were meant to increase the prowess of the current bouncer for the job. Gena, who'd recently won a blue band for karate, like to pose on that bed, sitting there, arms folded, relaxed and strained at once, showing the outline of those laurelled muscles.

There was a calendar for 1992 in the café with a picture of a chimpanzee who had weightlifter's deltoids, a denim waistcoat on him, denim jeans, chains snapped at his feet and beer in his fist.

Apart from the café, in which everyone seemed to be drunk, food a licence for as much alcohol as you could afford, there was also a coffee bar and a cinema upstairs which were part of the territory Gena protected.

Denis's mother had made a tiered, pale blue cake, with brown railings on its parapets, for New Year's Eve and the Christmas tree had hazy pink lights on it.

As Denis and his friends bopped to further rockabilly music from the cassette player during an interval in the kitchen, in a room with a poster for an appearance by the King in the Hector Piece Auditorium, Jackson, Florida, 1954, I looked through a box of photographs. Denis's mother was from Latvia.

There were photographs of outdoor summer funerals in Latvia, men with goatees and women in scarves facing the camera in a meadow outside a house, funeral processions along village streets in Latvia – the lid carried separately from the open casket. Photographs of funerals in pine forests, women converging with wreaths and potted plants. Gold-brown photographs of soldiers playing guitars, fishing. Photographs of women feeding leaves to gargoyles. Many photographs taken at shooting galleries. An old man with a large hooked nose dressed up as a pregnant woman. Then a photograph of him lying dead in a coffin, a religious band on his forehead. A photograph of another man lying dead with cloth petals strewn all around his head. Photographs of Denis on a cow at a summer house at Pavlovsk.

I'd met Denis at the Jazz Club early last summer. 'You're different from the other Englishmen,' he'd told me. 'You walk different.'

But almost everything I knew in St Petersburg was elusive and most stopovers had to be abruptly terminated.

A little Christmas tree in a kiosk deep in a metro had decorations of sweetpapers on it and at the top of the escalator three young women, one with a guitar, carolled the New Year, facing one another.

Before midnight I arrived at the party of my friend Dema, on Lomonosova Street. He'd given up his apartment two weeks before, was sleeping now in a bed near his friend Julia – 'But she is not my sexy friend' – had spent four thousand roubles hiring a studio for a week, erecting lasers in two rooms, just so he could give a New Year celebration to his friends.

In the first room I entered at a quarter to midnight young people were seated around two narrow tables stuck together to give the feeling of length and banquet. On the tables were vodka, London Dry Gin, Viennese beer, chocolate biscuits, clementines in a paper bag.

At midnight no embraces; just the clinking of glasses.

'On the outside I'm all smiles, a piece of theatre,' a girl called Katya told me, 'but inside I sob and sob. I'm thinking of my grandmother who's spending New Year alone. She could not get bread for the New Year. In the days of Stalin and Brezhnev you could get bread she says.'

Katya visits Germany often, on the invitation of her boyfriend who works in a Rudolf Steiner school in Essen. The Rudolf Steiner people, she said, believe the second coming will be in Russia and they come frequently, scouting for its signs. As Katya spoke I remembered what Steiner said about evil people, that you must become a diviner to protect yourself from them, divine the signs and intercept the blows.

This room was fire and divination now, and the streets I'd passed through, the colour of Imperial face paint, frequently screens for murder and starvation or mere statutory spiritual nihilism, were all part of a girl's improvisation now.

The dancing commenced in the other rooms and the lasers beamed and jetted and little nervous red dots flashed on the walls and two small Armenians arrived, the landlords, to inspect their premises and the party. They took one look at me and said I was a foreigner and shouldn't be there.

In Dema's previous flat, before he left it, the landlady – who he said looked like an otter – had started to move in, often staying for nights, choosing a variety of rooms as a bedroom.

I walked the streets. Before I'd left the party Dema had been wandering around, jacket thrown over his shoulder, white shirt seen to effect, a smile on that face which had a series of moles like beauty spots, his fringe truncated with a shears-like effect. In Dvortsovaya Square a woman dressed as a candy-pink pussycat pranced around on a stage. Little old ladies blew up balloons. People entangled with one another with streamers and tinsel. Into the early hours of the morning there were parties on stationary trams, girls emerging from the driver's compartment, pulling back their coats to show they had no skirts on.

A woman, her eyes violet from drink, came up and gave me a chocolate sweet, first holding it up as if it contained the transformative powers I needed.

On New Year's Day the lights on Nevsky Prospect went off for a while and people milled in the darkness. Then they came on; pale pink star flowers under a tray holding a huge fake bottle of champagne; little cylindrical lights on a little Christmas tree, blue, green, yellow and raspberry red; rims of shadow running through an arch of white bulbs at the entrance to a cinema; a quartet of shapes two blue, two white, juggling outside another cinema.

There was a spate of saucy cartoon nude ladies displayed outside cinemas on Nevsky Prospect; overweight bottoms, cherry nipples.

In the window of an ice-cream parlour an orange Santa carried a blue handbag in one hand and an orange-brown squirrel in the other.

Some sex maniac had daubed a poster on a wall, a nude girl crawling through the snow to a naked warrior flanked by wolves.

On 2 January the weather didn't know what to do with itself, halfway between fading snow and incipient mildness. People stood around in huddles, not knowing what to do with themselves. Trams looked as if they were about to die. And those big fur hats on people's heads seemed to stabilize the disarray, giving some people a druidic wisdom.

I visited two friends, a young married couple, on Kuznechnyy Lane. One was a television script writer, the other a translator. The walls were sparse, one picture against the Chinese red wallpaper, a very vicious-looking bear mauling some Napoleonic soldiers. There were photographs of a beloved silvery-haired aunt sneaked into the bookshelves which were epidemic in the apartment, in one her legs apart as she sat on a park bench and a pair of Oxfords on her feet. She'd recently died. In another photograph, elevated on the bookshelves, she hugged a bunch of carnations tipped by gold and red and blue. She'd never been to England but she'd spoken and taught English in an upper-class English accent learnt from one of those Edwardian governesses who inhabit the back of pre-revolutionary St Petersburg photographs. That accent had been passed to my friends.

We had a meal of barley porridge and tea.

On the table was my detritus of gifts.

My friend had just got up from bed, had thrown on a mauve jersey. Her head was bowed and she seemed to speak into the table as she said: 'There's just no food. All you can think of all the time is food, how to get it.'

I saw old ladies feed bread to pigeons that day and then walk away, mumbling to themselves, a set of silver teeth suddenly turning to you. I saw a newlywed couple lay flowers by the statue of Lieutenant Shmidta, a big rusted ship situated near him, on the other side a confectionary-type lavatory, one side for men, one side for women, the bride's veil blowing up like gossamer against all the other gossamer effects, the sheaths of snow on the aborigine-black shadow of St Isaac's, against the Neva which on the far side was like the surface of the moon, snow tufted on it, other parts clear, just pebbles of snow reinforcing the ebony.

That day Dema paid one rouble, fifty-five kopeks for milk which had previously been thirty-one kopeks, and two roubles, sixty kopeks for a loaf and a half of bread which would have previously cost sixty kopeks.

After the Jazz Club I visited a flat in student dorms near the Fontanka Canal with Dema. Two beds close by, a mattress in between, a mother from Stepnagorsk in one of the beds who'd brought big jars of strawberry jam she'd made which we kept dolloping on to biscuits, having tracked down the awakening freshness of last summer in the jam, a Christmas tree precipitously at the head of the flaxen-haired boy from Kaliningrad on the mattress who, when he heard me admiring his paintings and drawings which were pinned around, rose and with an iridescence in his blue eyes which made them even clearer presented me with a painting and a drawing.

In the kitchen on the other side of the corridor there was a different feast: dozens and dozens of insects on the wall around heaps of rubbish at the entrance to the kitchen.

On the evening of 4 January I met up with Dema again and some of his friends, Julia, Denis, another Dema, that Dema's thirteen-year-old daughter Kszniy.

'Money. But what does money matter? I don't think of money,' said Julia who, with the same leopardskin foulard at her neck over the same brown trouser suit she'd worn at Dema's party, looked like an escapee from a Toulouse-Lautrec painting. She had the conspiratorial feeling of an recent escapee too and seemed to find a similiar, manifest kind of conspiracy in me.

We drove around in Denis's father's Lada at first, then had tea and champagne in the second Dema's apartment, afterwards drove around again.

The second Dema was an artist and an architect who visits Germany often. My second night in St Petersburg this time I'd sat with him and some of his friends around the table in his apartment, glass on the table, covering a collection of old Soviet postcards in which Russian people who were made to look like kewpie dolls fondled one another, kissed, stared into one another's eyes under summer moons in indigo skies, on daytime park benches, on beaches. There was one odd card which looked like a British humorous one, a big woman in a saffron coat and little black pellet-hat hugging her tiny husband goodbye before taking the Leningrad–Sochi train.

As the others spoke in Russian I looked through a book of Soviet art and, inevitably, a portrait of Akhmatova came up, a profile by the artist Tyrsa.

These apartments, with dual-coloured walls leading to them, with their mess like pigs' feed outside the doors, with their air of attrition at the entrances, reminded me of apartments in Dublin and Cork.

'You can live with your history,' I'd said on my first visit. 'Much as I love the cities of Dublin and Cork I've got to escape them.'

The two Demas tipped glasses before parting that first night, towards this, 'their first meeting'.

In the hotel room I was sharing with an Englishman, after that late social night which, as after a Galway party in one of my stories, left a strange colour, 'like light in wine or a reflection on a saxophone', I was vindictively woken by the World Service at eight in the morning.

Denis, whom I met for the first time on 4 January, had the fragile face of an overgrown child and a child's quizzical sense of wanting to know all the time if he was doing the right thing even if he was doing nothing. He wore French oyster-white jeans. He'd lived in France for a year, supported by someone – he didn't say if it was a woman or a man. But under these circumstances he'd clashed with something in himself. He demonstrated the kind of collision by veering his flat down-turned hand against an empty German champagne bottle. His hand impacted with my wrist in the process and paused, as if to feel what I knew of the situation, and seemed to detect the electricity of a similiar, even greater clash, a clash with the patriarchal God and the secretively gleaming Mother of the Russian Orthodox church maybe, before going on.

Under the auspices of a sense of these deities he'd got the Paris–Moscow train back to Russia for a pause.

But he was too young to be a stone yet. He'd return to France soon.

He spoke about France as if it were an understanding friend and I remembered hitchhiking with a lemon-haired girl from Dublin on the Riviera at night, cars stopping and the drivers inquiring: '*Voulez vous faire l'amour tout les deux?*' I remembered the first time I saw grapes growing, with this girl, old women touching the azure-ash clusters from beneath.

Boats docked by the Neva are decorated with strings of white lights as we drive around. It was my fifth visit to St Petersburg in three years. I came here to find Dublin and Cork and also to be away from the racist country in which I was shacked.

Against a lighted boat Denis put his arms about me and said: 'I know there are bad people. But take it easy, man.'

I knew who he was then. He was an orphan in the convent in Ballinasloe when I was a child who reputedly had a Russian father and who would stand endlessly in the convent grounds against the river Suck in the cornflower-blue orphan's outfit.

Back in the racist country again, without St Petersburg, I felt the emptiness like never before.

> He wanders through deserted rooms
> And tidies up for hours.[1]

[1] Boris Pasternak, tr. Lydia P. Slater